THIS PAGE:
The Big Room, Carlsbad Caverns NP.

ON THE COVER:
Stalactites and draperies decorate the Dome
Room, Carlsbad Caverns NP

Photos by: Ronal Kerbo

Carlsbad Caverns National Park

Geologic Resource Evaluation Report

Natural Resource Report NPS/NRPC/GRD/NRR—2007/003

Geologic Resources Division
Natural Resource Program Center
P.O. Box 25287
Denver, Colorado 80225

June 2007

U.S. Department of the Interior
Washington, D.C.

The Natural Resource Publication series addresses natural resource topics that are of interest and applicability to a broad readership in the National Park Service and to others in the management of natural resources, including the scientific community, the public, and the NPS conservation and environmental constituencies. Manuscripts are peer- reviewed to ensure that the information is scientifically credible, technically accurate, appropriately written for the intended audience, and is designed and published in a professional manner.

Natural Resource Reports are the designated medium for disseminating high priority, current natural resource management information with managerial application. The series targets a general, diverse audience, and may contain NPS policy considerations or address sensitive issues of management applicability. Examples of the diverse array of reports published in this series include vital signs monitoring plans; "how to" resource management papers; proceedings of resource management workshops or conferences; annual reports of resource programs or divisions of the Natural Resource Program Center; resource action plans; fact sheets; and regularly- published newsletters.

Views and conclusions in this report are those of the authors and do not necessarily reflect policies of the National Park Service. Mention of trade names or commercial products does not constitute endorsement or recommendation for use by the National Park Service.

Printed copies of reports in these series may be produced in a limited quantity and they are only available as long as the supply lasts. This report is also available from the Geologic Resource Evaluation Program website (http://www2.nature.nps.gov/geology/inventory/gre_publications) on the internet, or by sending a request to the address on the back cover. Please cite this publication as:

Graham, J. 2007. Carlsbad Caverns National Park Geologic Resource Evaluation Report. Natural Resource Report NPS/NRPC/GRD/NRR—2007/003. National Park Service, Denver, Colorado.

NPS D- 139, June 2007

Table of Contents

List of Figures

List of Tables

Executive Summary

This report has been developed to accompany the digital geologic map produced by Geologic Resource Evaluation staff for Carlsbad Caverns National Park. It contains information relevant to resource management and scientific research.

Established as a unit of the National Park System in 1923, Carlsbad Caverns National Park preserves Carlsbad Caverns and numerous other caves within an ancient fossil reef while protecting an extraordinary and unique ecological association of bats, cave climate, speleothems, hydrology, cave fauna, and microbes. In 1995, the United Nations recognized the worldwide significance of the spectacular natural resources at Carlsbad Caverns National Park by designating it as a World Heritage Site. Preservation and management of the geologic resources are important for enhancement of the visitor's experience and sustenance of the ecosystem.

Over 300 caves are known in the Guadalupe Mountains, and more than 100 caves have been surveyed inside the boundary of Carlsbad Caverns National Park. Decorations in these caves are arguably unsurpassed in the world and include dazzling gypsum chandeliers, sheet-like draperies, towering columns and domes, delicate soda-straw stalactites and other speleothems of great abundance and variation. The Big Room is the largest cave chamber in North America.

Carlsbad Caverns is also an extraordinary example of aggressive sulfuric acid dissolution. Most of the world's caves have developed through dissolution of limestone by weak carbonic acid, a by-product of meteoric groundwater and carbon dioxide. At Carlsbad Caverns, hydrogen sulfide migrated upward from deeply buried petroleum reservoirs and reacted with groundwater, forming sulfuric acid, dissolving the Capitan Limestone.

The dramatic landscape of the park is part of the Guadalupe Mountains, a mountain range recognized as the best-preserved Permian fossil reef in the world. Reef limestones form the prominent Guadalupe Escarpment and back-reef carbonates form the canyons and plateaus to the northwest. Geologists from all over the world come to the Guadalupe Mountains to study this Permian reef complex.

Carlsbad Caverns National Park lies just 5 miles (8 km) north of Guadalupe Mountains National Park along Guadalupe ridge. Each year over 500,000 visitors place increasing demands on the resources of Carlsbad Caverns.

The following issues, features, and processes were identified at scoping sessions as having critical management significance to the park:

- Water contamination: Infiltration of contaminated water from parking lots and sewer lines has the potential to impact the entire ecosystem, destroying cave features and the habitat of the world-famous colony of migratory Mexican free-tailed bats. This situation has resulted in the re-evaluation of infrastructure above the cave and measures to prevent contaminated water from entering the cave.

- Cave preservation: Caves contain delicate non-renewable resources and are a component of fragile karstic eco-systems. The continual use, development, and exploration of caves can have an extremely detrimental impact on those resources and eco-systems. Food, chewing gum, litter, lint, and urine are left behind by visitors to the developed caves as well as the undeveloped caves of the park. In the past, as many as 2,000 speleothems each year were vandalized or stolen from Carlsbad Cavern. Measures are being taken to reduce human impacts to park caves. One such measure has been the implementation of strict rules that cavers must follow to prevent the destruction of cave features and native microbes in Lechuguilla Cave.

- Water supply and Rattlesnake Springs: Rattlesnake Springs is the sole water supply source for the park and provides a vital wetland habitat for several species of threatened birds and fish. Contamination of the groundwater and groundwater flow paths continue to be management concerns.

- External mineral extraction and associated hazards: Carlsbad Caverns is surrounded by active hydrocarbon exploration that could have a negative impact on cave resources. The extraction of mineral commodities such as potash also occurs in the vicinity of the park.

- Paleontological resources: Marine invertebrate fossils are critical to the determination of Permian reef environments, and the identification of surface exposures at Carlsbad Caverns. These fossils provide a remarkable outdoor laboratory to study this ancient ecosystem. In addition, exemplary Pleistocene fossils are found in several of the caves at the park. Preservation and protection of paleontological resources from theft and destruction is critical to maintaining their scientific value and the visitor experience.

- Bat habitat: The survival of the park's population of migratory Mexican free-tailed bats depends upon understanding the relationship between geology and the environment.

Introduction

The following section briefly describes the regional geologic setting and the National Park Service Geologic Resource Evaluation Program.

Purpose of the Geologic Resources Evaluation Program

The Geologic Resource Evaluation (GRE) Program is one of 12 inventories funded under the NPS Natural Resource Challenge designed to enhance baseline information available to park managers. The program carries out the geologic component of the inventory effort from the development of digital geologic maps to providing park staff with a geologic report tailored to a park's specific geologic resource issues. The Geologic Resources Division of the Natural Resource Program Center administers this program. The GRE team relies heavily on partnerships with the U.S. Geological Survey, Colorado State University, state surveys, and others in developing GRE products.

The goal of the GRE Program is to increase understanding of the geologic processes at work in parks and provide sound geologic information for use in park decision making. Sound park stewardship relies on understanding natural resources and their role in the ecosystem. Geology is the foundation of park ecosystems. The compilation and use of natural resource information by park managers is called for in section 204 of the National Parks Omnibus Management Act of 1998 and in NPS-75, Natural Resources Inventory and Monitoring Guideline.

To realize this goal, the GRE team is systematically working towards providing each of the identified 270 natural area parks with a geologic scoping meeting, a digital geologic map, and a geologic report. These products support the stewardship of park resources and are designed for non-geoscientists. During scoping meetings the GRE team brings together park staff and geologic experts to review available geologic maps and discuss specific geologic issues, features, and processes. Scoping meetings are usually held for individual parks and on occasion for an entire Vital Signs Monitoring Network. The GRE mapping team converts the geologic maps identified for park use at the scoping meeting into digital geologic data in accordance with their innovative Geographic Information Systems (GIS) Data Model. These digital data sets bring an exciting interactive dimension to traditional paper maps by providing geologic data for use in park GIS and facilitating the incorporation of geologic considerations into a wide range of resource management applications. The newest maps come complete with interactive help files. As a companion to the digital geologic maps, the GRE team prepares a park-specific geologic report that aids in use of the maps and provides park managers with an overview of park geology and geologic resource management issues.

For additional information regarding the content of this report and up to date GRE contact information please refer to the Geologic Resource Evaluation web site (http://www2.nature.nps.gov/geology/inventory/).

Regional Description

Carlsbad Caverns National Park, was proclaimed a national monument in 1923 and established as a national park in 1930. The park preserves over 100 known caves formed within a Permian-age fossil reef in southeastern New Mexico. One of the major cave systems in the park, Lechuguilla Cave, is the nation's deepest limestone cave (1,593 feet [486 m]) and the third longest. Lechuguilla contains speleothems and microbes found nowhere else in the world. The Big Room in Carlsbad Cavern is the largest, most easily accessible chamber in North America. The United Nations recognized the worldwide significance of the natural resources at Carlsbad Caverns National Park by designating the park a World Heritage Site in 1995.

Located less than 5 miles (8 km) north of Guadalupe Mountains National Park and about 20 miles (32 km) southwest of Carlsbad, New Mexico, Carlsbad Caverns National Park incorporates 46,766 acres in two separate units (figure 1) (NPS 1996). The main unit extends for about 21 miles (34 km) southwestward along the Capitan Reef and varies from 3 to 6 miles (5 to 10 km) wide. This unit contains the cavern that gives the park its name and most of the park development, which was built on top of the reef escarpment. The backcountry stretches for miles to the west and south and includes the escarpment and several deeply cut canyons.

The separate Rattlesnake Springs unit contains about 80 acres and lies 7 miles (11 km) southwest of the park entrance. Rattlesnake Springs is the source of the park's water supply.

Elevations in the park range from 3,596 feet (1,096 m) in the lowlands to 6,368 feet (1,941 m) on the escarpment. About 71 percent of the park (33,125 acres) is designated wilderness and is managed according to the provisions of the Wilderness Act and NPS wilderness policies.

Carlsbad Caverns is rich not only in geologic history but also with cultural resources reflecting a long and varied history of human occupation. This history attests to the ability of humans to adapt to the harsh Chihuahuan Desert environment. About one million artifacts are preserved and protected in the park museum. These artifacts represent prehistoric and historic Native American occupations, European exploration and settlement, industrial exploitation, commercial and cavern accessibility development, and tourism, which have each left their mark on the area. Two historic districts, the Cavern Historic District and the Rattlesnake

Springs Historic District, are on the National Register of Historic Places.

General Geology

Carlsbad Caverns National Park is located within the Guadalupe Mountains, a limestone mountain range recognized as the best-preserved Permian-aged fossil reef in the world. The fossils here reveal a detailed picture of life along the coastline of a shallow inland sea 240 – 280 million years ago. Eventually, the coastline became a horseshoe-shaped limestone layer of rock over 1,800 ft (550 m) thick, 2 – 3 mi (3 – 5 km) wide and over 400 mi (640 km) long that bordered the Delaware Basin (figure 2). The Delaware and Midland basins are part of the Permian Basin, one of the most productive petroleum provinces in North America.

By the end of the Permian age sediments thousands of feet thick covered the Capitan reef burying it for tens of millions of years. Local faulting and stresses, especially over the past 20 million years, uplifted these reef sediments almost 10,000 feet (3,000 m) and tilted the uplifted block to the east. Wind, rain, and snow have since eroded away the overlying rock exposing the ancient reef to the surface once again. The reef limestones now form the prominent Guadalupe Escarpment, a physiographic feature oriented northeast-southwest. The deep canyons and caves of Carlsbad Caverns allow visitors to view this Permian reef from the inside.

The Permian stratigraphic section at the park records back-reef, reef, and fore-reef environments (figure 3). Fine-grained layers of siltstone in the back-reef strata are low permeability barriers to groundwater flow and provide a cap rock against further erosion (Van der Heijde et al. 1997). Along with brecciated fore-reef limestones, cavernous, fractured, massive reef limestones constitute the Capitan Formation.

The Guadalupe Mountains contain over 300 known caves and more than 100 have been surveyed inside Carlsbad Caverns National Park (NPS fact sheet 2005). Many of these caves exhibit the characteristically large rooms associated with sulfuric acid dissolution. The 370-ft (113 m)-high, 14-acre Big Room in Carlsbad Caverns, for example, is the largest cave chamber in North America (Kiver and Harris 1999).

At present, Carlsbad Cavern is relatively dry due to the arid nature of the surface climate. The dripping heard today inside the cavern is only an echo of what would have been heard during prior, wetter times. If in the future, the climate becomes wetter the growth of speleothems will accelerate, conversely a more arid environment will slow speleothem growth.

Park History

Stories have it that in the late 1800s James Larkin White, a local cowboy in southeastern New Mexico, investigated a column of "smoke" and found millions of bats emerging from a huge hole in the ground. This became known as "Bat Cave." Bat Cave was later named Carlsbad Cave before becoming Carlsbad Cavern. Seeking a profit, miners staked claims and removed over 100,000 tons of bat guano, an extremely rich fertilizer, from Carlsbad and other Guadalupe Mountains caves from 1901 – 1921. The guano was shipped to the citrus groves in California. The floor of Bat Cave was lowered by as much as 50 feet (15 m), but none of the companies selling bat guano were profitable (Kiver and Harris 1999).

During the early 1900s, Jim White was working as a guano miner and began to explore the cave and guide interested people into the lower chambers. On one of these tours, Robert Halley of the General Land Office, Department of the Interior, was so impressed with the beauty of the caverns that his report led President Coolidge to establish Carlsbad Caverns as a national monument in 1923. In 1924, an article written by Willis T. Lee, a noted U.S. Geological Survey geologist who had led a 6-month National Geographic expedition to the cave, appeared in National Geographic magazine. Lee's article led to increased public interest and the subsequent elevation to national park status in 1930.

Exploration of the caves at Carlsbad Caverns National Park continues to enrich the park's history. Over a period of 2 years, a group of cave explorers slowly removed rubble from a blocked passage in a cave about 3 miles (4.8 km) from the entrance to Carlsbad Cavern. A strong flow of air indicated that more passages probably existed beyond the blocked passage. In 1986, explorers finished digging out the rubble and found the incredible depths of Lechuguilla Cave.

Jim White, the first explorer and unofficial guide to the cave, later became a park ranger and advanced to chief ranger. He devoted his life to opening up an underground wonderland that is now enjoyed by nearly one million visitors from all over the world each year.

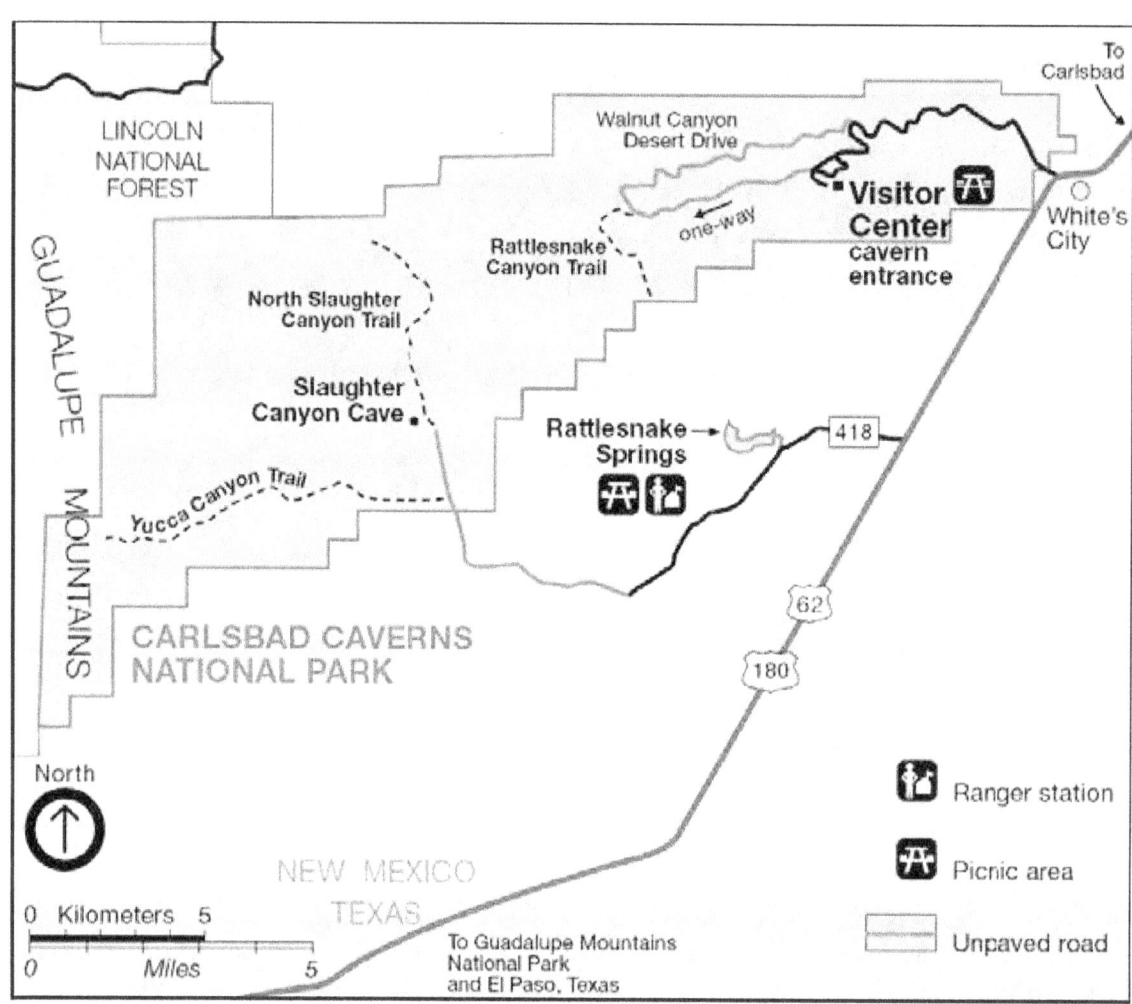

Figure 1. Location map of Carlsbad Caverns National Park.

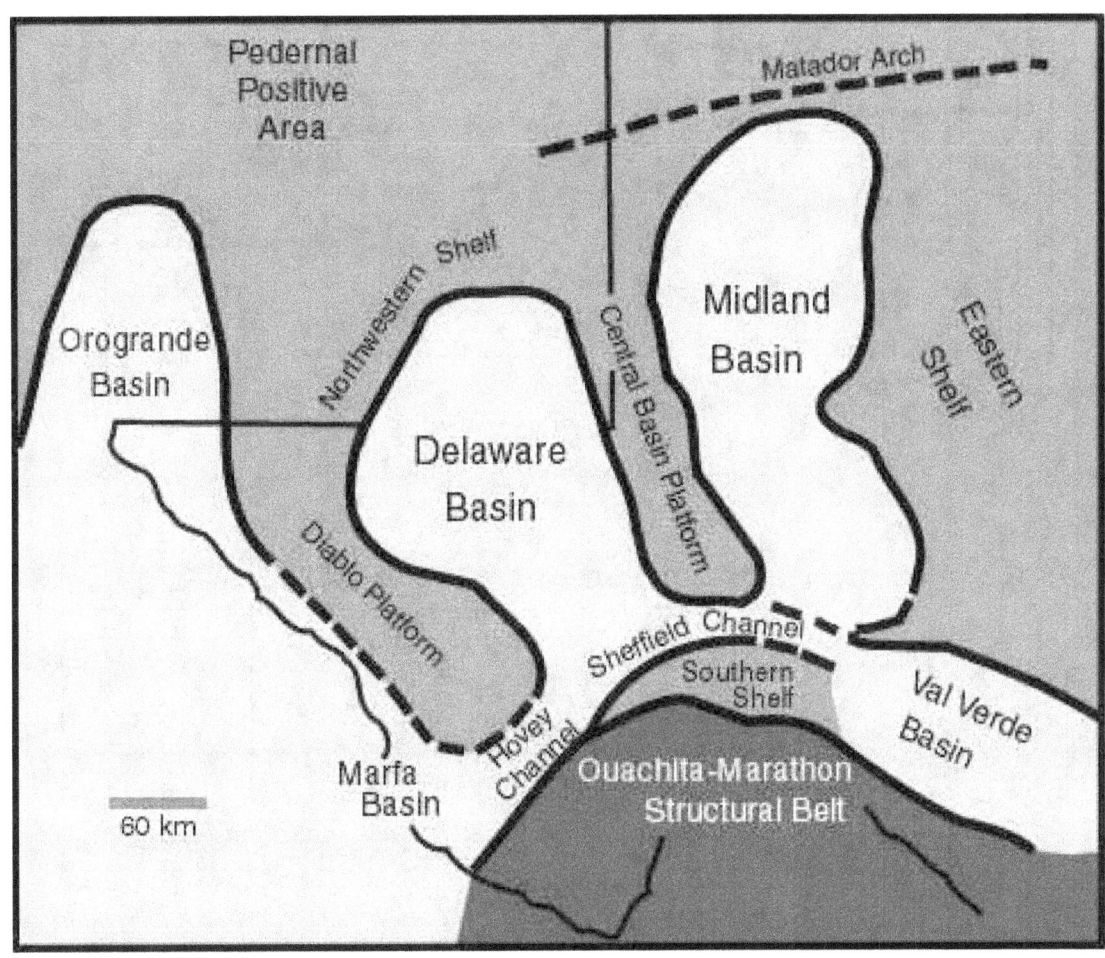

Figure 2. Major physiographic features of the Permian Basin during early Guadalupian time. Diagram from the New Mexico Institute of Mining and Geology, http://www.geoinfo.nmt.edu/staff/scholle/guadalupe.html#genset (accessed 2005.)

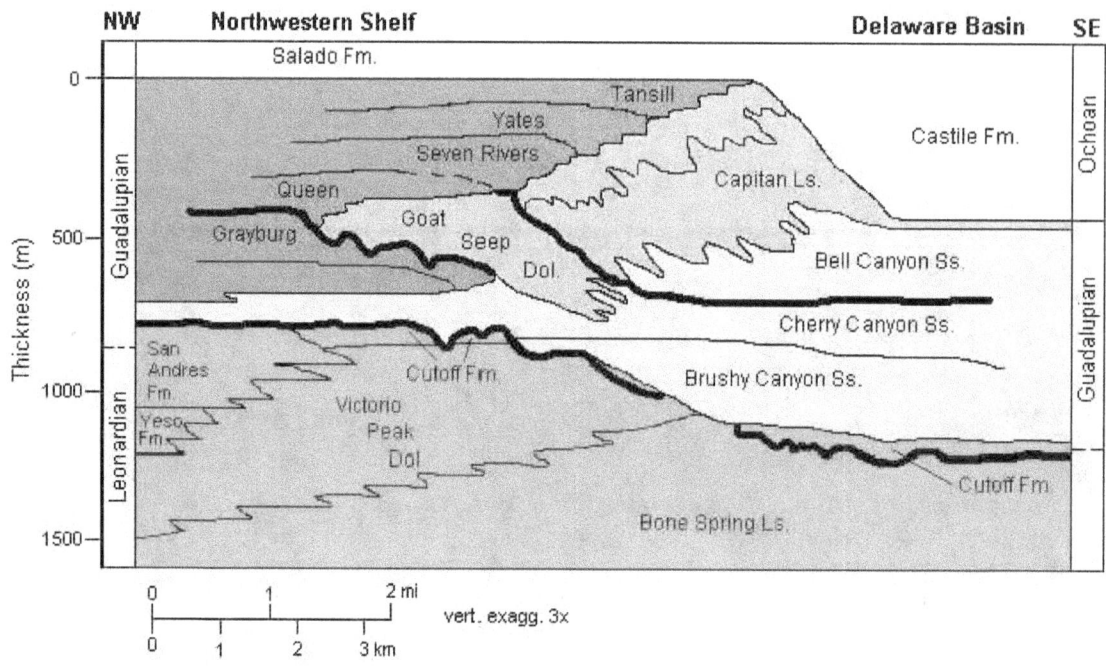

Period	Epoch	Back Reef Strata	Reef Strata	Fore Reef and Basin Strata
PERMIAN	Ochoa		Capitan Limestone	Rustler Fm
				Castile Fm
	Guadalupe	Tansill Fm		Bell Canyon Fm
		Yates Fm		
		Seven Rivers Fm		
		Queen Fm	Goat Seep Dolomite	Cherry Canyon Formation
		Grayburg Fm		
	Leonard	Sandstone tongue of Cherry Canyon Fm		
		San Andres Formation		

B)

Figure 3. Schematic cross-section (A) and stratigraphic column (B) for Carlsbad Cavern National Park showing back-reef, reef, and fore-reef formations. Colored formations in (B) are present within Carlsbad Caverns. Thick black lines in (A) are surfaces of erosion.

Geologic Issues

A Geologic Resource Evaluation scoping session was held for Carlsbad Caverns National Park on March 6-8, 2001, to discuss geologic resources, to address the status of geologic mapping, and to assess resource management issues and needs. The following section synthesizes the scoping results, in particular, those issues that may require attention from resource managers.

Significant geologic resources exposed both at the surface and in the caves pose geologic issues for the resource manager. Discussions during a one-day field trip, and the in-house scoping session, as well as from the *Final General Management Plan/Environmental Impact Statement* (GMP/EIS) identify the following geologic issues for Carlsbad Caverns National Park.

Water Contamination

Factors contributing to a relatively high vulnerability of Carlsbad Cavern National Park caves to contamination from the surface include: 1) the absence of a significant, continuous soil zone over the cave system, 2) the presence of localized but highly permeable fracture zones in the limestone, and 3) the presence of well developed karst. Most of the contaminants from parking lots are carried by the first 0.5 inch (13 mm) of rain. About 540,000 liters of contaminated water enters the groundwater system from parking lots in every 0.5 inch (13 mm) rainstorm. On average, there are 10 storms per year that produce more than 0.5 inch (13 mm) of rain (Bremer 1998). Therefore, at least 5.3 million liters of contaminated water enter the groundwater system every year (Burger and Pate 2001).

Studies by Brooke (1996) and van der Heijde and others (1997) identified three major potential sources that could threaten both water quality in the cavern and public health: 1) leaks in the sewer lines; 2) contaminated runoff from spills and vehicle fires on public parking lots and road segments; and 3) spills, leaking tanks, fires, and other accidental releases from the maintenance yard. The most threatened areas identified by the study in Carlsbad Cavern were: Quintessential Right, Left Hand Tunnel, New Section, the Main Corridor between Devil's Spring and Iceberg Rock, and locations in Chocolate High, the New Mexico Room, the Scenic Rooms, and the Big Room area (Van der Heijde et al. 1997). Infiltration in the vadose zone from the surface to the caves varies between 4 to 10 years in the Main Corridor and 14 to 35 years in the Big Room.

Infiltration research led to a re-evaluation of the infrastructure above the cave and proposals to change the management of cave and karst resources in the park (Burger and Pate 2001). Modifications of the developed area above Carlsbad Caverns were proposed in order to: 1) protect groundwater and cave resources from continuing chronic exposure to contamination, 2) protect cave resources from potential catastrophic contamination, and 3) protect visitors to Carlsbad

Caverns from potential hazardous conditions due to contamination. The park prepared an Environmental Assessment (EA) designed to reduce the impacts from park facilities on the cave. Recommendations included the following proposals (Burger and Pate 2001; Pate personal communication 2006). Plans are currently in the works to replace the main outfall sewer line, remove most of the Bat Cave Draw Parking Lot, and install oil & grit separators on remaining lots. These changes are slated for implementation in the next 1 to 3 years (Pate personal communication 2006).

- Treat some of the runoff and eliminate some paved areas altogether.
- Resurface parking lots near the visitor center so that they drain southward, away from the cave.
- Install a storm water filtration system at drainage points for these parking lots
- Close the large parking lot in Bat Cave Draw to reduce the amount of vehicle fluid buildup. The EA recommends removing most of this parking lot and replacing it with a bus turnaround area and handicapped access path to the natural entrance
- Remove most of the paved surface and replace it with natural vegetation to help restore natural drainage and infiltration conditions.
- Replace the sewage collection system in the housing and office area north of Bat Cave Draw with new lines.
- Reroute the main sewage line southward to minimize the exposure of the caves to sewage leaks.

Sewage line repair and restructuring of the parking lots are funding priorities for the park. Implementation of a space reallocation plan would remove most residents from above the cave thus reducing the amount of sewage in the system and the number of vehicles parked above the cave on the north side of Bat Cave Draw.

Cave Preservation

Several anthropogenic structures located within the subsurface may affect the amount and distribution of water infiltrating into and through the subsurface. Water percolating into the subsurface is redistributed by the extensive underground trail system and virtually impervious lunchroom area about 750 feet (250 m) below the visitor's center (Van der Heijde et al. 1997). In the past, periodic cleaning of the trails released water into the surrounding caverns. Water lines along the trails are no longer in use but remain in the cave and could leak at an unknown rate at connection points and at spigots if use was resumed (Brooke 1996; Pate personal communication 2006). In the past, runoff from trails was thought to contain rock fragments, organic compounds, and nitrates from urine on the trail (Van der Heijde et al. 1997). However, trails in the cave are no longer washed so contaminated water is not released into the cave environment (Pate personal communication 2006).

The elevator and utility shafts underneath the visitor's center also provide major downward conduits for water infiltrating the upper formations (Brooke 1996). A sewage pump removes wastewater from the restroom facilities located within the lunchroom area through the utility shaft to the surface. Equipment failure or maintenance practices of these restroom and sewage transport facilities may result in contamination. Recognition of problems with the current pump and standpipe has prompted the park to request money for their replacement. However, the timeline for implementation of a new system remains uncertain (Pate personal communication 2006).

More than 500,000 visitors a year enter Carlsbad Caverns. Food, chewing gum, litter, and lint have been found throughout the cavern. Discoloration of speleothems in Carlsbad Caverns results from large accumulations of lint, clothing fibers, dead skin, and hair left behind each year by thousands of cave visitors. The buildup of lint makes the speleothems appear dull and gray. Investigations show that lint is a very good source of organic material for microbes, mites, and spiders and that the breakdown of the lint may generate organic acids that dissolve calcite speleothems (Burger and Pate 2001).

Researchers found that short rock walls along the sides of the trail contain much of the lint. To reduce lint accumulations, rock walls have been and are continuing to be, built along the five-kilometer-long trail (Pate personal communication 2006). The trail is vacuumed twice a year to remove lint and a volunteer group works in the cave during an annual week-long "Lint Camp" to remove lint and other litter from along the visitor trail system.

Formerly water was used to clean the floor in areas where there is a problem with visitors urinating in the cave and in places where the trail may become slick (Burger and Pate 2001). However, runoff from this cleaning method was problematic and as a result a new method of cleaning has been adopted. The new method of cleaning problem areas involves applying a bleach solution that is then covered with an absorbent material and removed from the cave. This has eliminated the presence of contaminated runoff from trail cleaning in the cave (Pate personal communication 2006).

Speleothem breakage monitoring between 1985 and 1991 revealed that as many as 2,000 speleothems annually were vandalized or stolen. Measures taken to correct this problem included the addition of stainless steel railings along both sides of the paved trail through the self-guided portions of the cave. During the installation of the railings from 1997 to 2000, monitoring showed that visitors leaving the trail system declined significantly. This monitoring also appeared to show a significant slow in vandalism to speleothems. Nevertheless, vandalism remains a concern and an ongoing problem for resource management (Pate personal communication 2006).

Lights in the cavern create an environment that allows algae, moss, and fungus to grow. The lights also draw animals farther into the cave than they would normally venture. These factors impact and change the cave environment.

Although entry to Lechuguilla Cave requires a permit, exploration and research have resulted in some adverse impacts to pristine cave resources. In 1996 it was documented that opening the lid to the airlock-culvert system allowed small dirt and debris particles to fall into the cave, and created a blast of air that was thought to affect cave conditions. The installation of a stainless steel access tube with an airlock system has corrected the problems associated with debris and airflow at the entrance (Pate personal communication 2006).

Expeditions requiring several days are necessary to explore and precisely document new areas, but exploration, recording expeditions, and careless travel have damaged numerous formations. Many delicate and once pristine formations adjacent to travel routes are covered by mud and dirt. The park has addressed this by implementing more stringent guidelines, including the requirement that minimum impact caving techniques be used when working in the cave. This action has led to better overall protection of cave resources. In addition restoration activities have also corrected some of the more serious impacts (Pate personal communication 2006).

Human urine also impacts the cave environment (NPS 1996). For safety and ultimately the protection of cave resources, urine is allowed to be placed in designated locations in the cave when expeditions require more than two days. This remains one of the more serious impacts to the cave environment despite various researchers' efforts to solve this difficult problem (Pate personal communication 2006).

As of 2006, 113 caves are known in the park. Although, cave resources in the backcountry are not being fully monitored, there is little evidence of vandalism and theft of cave resources.

Several caves outside the park boundary on U.S. Forest Service (USFS) and Bureau of Land Management (BLM) lands might connect to pristine park caves such as Lechuguilla and possibly other undiscovered caves (NPS 1996). Many water sources that are integral to the formation of the caves and ecosystem in the park also originate outside the park boundary.

Water Supply and Rattlesnake Springs
Rattlesnake Springs lies south of Guadalupe Ridge, about 5 miles (8 km) from the mouth of Slaughter Canyon, and

is the sole water supply source for Carlsbad Caverns National Park. It also provides a vital wetland habitat that supports several species of threatened birds and fish.

In 1948, the National Park Service became concerned about aquifer contamination when agricultural development began. There is evidence showing that an aquifer adjacent to the one that supplies water to Rattlesnake Springs has been contaminated by oil and gas activities and that high flow conditions spill this contaminated water over into the Rattlesnake Springs drainage area (Pate personal communication 2006). A nearby gas field produces from the Morrow Formation (Pennsylvanian), the most important natural gas producer in the Delaware Basin of southeastern New Mexico (Mazzullo and Brister 2001). If there is a breach in the casing, a loss of circulation, or another drilling problem, the result could be contamination of one or more of the aquifers that supply water to the park and surrounding landowners. Because of these concerns, the National Park Service sponsored a study of the aquifer supplying Rattlesnake Springs (Bowen 1998).

Rattlesnake Springs is a high-discharge artesian spring that flows from a karstic, well-indurated limestone conglomerate located at the distal end of a small alluvial wedge between the Gypsum Plain of the Delaware Basin and the Guadalupe Reef Escarpment. The conglomerate is derived from the large alluvial fan emanating from Slaughter Canyon and is either Miocene-Pliocene or Pleistocene in age (Bowen 1998).

The limestone conglomerate lies above the Castile Formation, a regional confining layer, or aquitard. The low conductivity of the Castile is due to the presence of evaporites that have some of the lowest conductivity of any natural media ($2x10^{-8}$ to $4x10^{-13}$ m/sec).

Based on hydrologic data, Bowen (1998) hypothesized that flow within the Slaughter Canyon alluvial fan "is controlled by karst channels within the limestone conglomerate." The heterogeneity of the system localizes flow within channels and isolates the conglomerate between finer silt- and clay-dominated sediments. Karstic channels produce mostly isolated, discrete flow paths, and these flow paths need to be identified for the Slaughter Canyon area. An electrical survey (ground penetrating radar) could be used to identify the channels.

Bowen (1998) concluded that contamination of Rattlesnake Springs was not likely to occur from the nearby Washington Ranch natural gas injection facility. Furthermore, current agricultural withdrawals from the system appeared to have minimal impact on Rattlesnake Springs. Bowen cautioned, however, that future developments of the upper Black River Valley "could have significant impacts on the system due to the karstic nature of flow" (Bowen 1998).

The NPS has recently funded a group out of the University of Texas at El Paso to accurately determine the location of the discreet channel (or channels) that feed Rattlesnake Springs. Once determined, any future

drilling for oil & gas can be directed away from this (or these) channels (Pate personal communication 2006).

Water flow in the park's backcountry springs and seeps has been monitored on an annual basis since the early 1960s. At that time 10 permanent springs, 12 permanent seeps, and 6 intermittent seeps were recorded. About half of these water sources were developed for early ranching and guano mining operations. Remnants of earthen and metal tanks, check dams, and catchment basins still exist. In 1993, 47 seeps and springs were inventoried in the park. About 20 of these are permanent water sources considered critical to wildlife.

Mineral Resources

Oil and Gas

Under federal law, no federal mineral or oil and gas leasing or the associated development is permissible in Carlsbad Caverns National Park. In addition, provisions in the Lechiguilla Cave Protection Act, the record of decision by the Bureau of Land Management with regard to the Bureau's *Dark Canyon Environmental Impact Statement* (establishing an 8,320-acre cave protection area north of Carlsbad Caverns National Park in the vicinity of Dark Canyon), and the USFS management action provide protection for many cave resources. However oil and gas are produced on state lands, and exploration and production on unrestricted state and private lands has the potential to irreparably alter or destroy cave resources in Carlsbad Caverns National Park.

The Lechuguilla Cave Protection Act (Public Law 103-169) gives additional protection to Lechuguilla Cave and other cave resources in and near the park by establishing a 9,720-acre cave protection area (NPS 1996). The act withdraws 6,280 acres of adjacent federal lands from mineral exploration and development and prohibits new drilling. However, the act does not apply to the 960 acres of adjacent private lands or 2,880 acres of state-owned lands within the cave protection area. Protective measures in the Lechuguilla Cave Protection Act include:

- Prohibiting occupancy on existing federal leases
- Canceling existing federal leases where necessary
- Prohibiting additional drilling on federal leases
- Limiting surface access to all federal leases in the cave protection area

During the summer of 2006 the State of New Mexico issued oil and gas leases on five sections of land approximately two miles north of the park boundary. These five sections of state land lie within the 9,720 acre cave protection area. No wells have been drilled in this state lease area at the time of this writing. Additional leasing on state and private lands north of the park remains a possibility. The NPS is trying to initiate a dialogue with the state of New Mexico to address park protection concerns.

Since the 1920's, hydrocarbon exploration has been active south of Carlsbad Caverns National Park in the Delaware Basin, a sub-basin of the larger Permian Basin. About 71 percent of Permian Basin oil (65 billion barrels) and 54 percent of Permian Basin associated and dissolved gas-in-place (0.93 trillion cu m; 32.7 trillion cu ft) have been produced from Permian-age strata. The remainder (mostly gas) is produced from Pennsylvanian or older Paleozoic rock, predominantly from the Ordovician Ellenburger Formation (Table 1) (Ward et al. 1986; Hill 1996).

TABLE 1: Producing units in the Delaware Basin

Period	Formation	Oil/Gas
Permian	Tansill Fm	Oil
	Yates Fm	Oil
	Seven Rivers Fm	Oil
	Queen Fm	Oil
	Grayburg Fm	Oil
	Bell Canyon Fm	Oil
	Cherry Creek Fm	Oil
	Brushy Canyon Fm	Oil
	San Andres Fm	Oil
	Abo-bone Spring	Oil
	Wolfcamp Fm	Oil
Pennsylvanian	Cisco Fm	Oil
	Canyon Fm	Oil
	Strawn Fm	Gas
	Atoka Fm	Gas
	Morrow Fm	Gas
Devonian	Woodford Fm	Gas
Silurian	Fusselman Fm	Gas
Ordovician	Montoya Fm	Gas
	Ellenburger Fm	Gas

(From Hill (1996) and the Texas Bureau of Economic Geology, access 2005)

The largest producers of oil in the Delaware (and Permian) Basin are the Guadalupian-age reservoirs of the Queen, Seven Rivers, Yates, and Tansill Formations (figure 3) (Ward et al. 1986; Hill 1996; New Mexico Institute of Mining and Technology 2005). Together, they account for 67 percent of all Permian oil found and 62 percent of all Permian gas found in the Delaware Basin. The second most prolific Permian reservoirs are found in Leonardian strata such as the open-shelf San Andreas Limestone (figure 4). Most of the production from Permian rocks comes from less than 5,000 feet (1,500 m) (Dolton et al. 1979).

Hydrocarbon traps in Permian rocks are mostly a combination of stratigraphic and structural traps with the hydrocarbons sealed in place by porosity and permeability barriers of carbonate, evaporite, or shale. Production is maximized in the near-back-reef or grainstone margin facies that was neither cemented like the reefs nor plugged with evaporite cement like back-reef strata closer to shore. Back-reef environments account for more than 90 percent of all hydrocarbon production in the Delaware Basin (figure 4).

No production comes from the Capitan, Victorio Peak, or Goat Seep reef or fore-reef facies. These rocks were tightly cemented on the sea floor shortly after deposition (New Mexico Institute of Mining and Technology 2005).

Basin sediments account for the rest of the production. Hydrocarbons are trapped in submarine channel sandstones and basinal limestones of the Delaware Mountain Group (Bell Canyon, Brushy Canyon, and Cherry Canyon Formations) (Berg 1979; Williamson 1979; Hill 1996; Texas Bureau of Economic Geology 2005). The submarine channel sandstones pinch out against the Capitan reef complex.

Most of the Permian oil is generated from the largely organic, carbon-rich, basinal sediments such as the Bone Spring Limestone. Oil in basinal facies has probably migrated only a short distance from source to reservoir. Oil in back-reef facies, however, moved up-section or laterally through fractured reef sediments to get from source to reservoir. Although cementation destroyed reef porosity, permeability through the reef zone was high due to fracturing of the reef.

Current estimates suggest that 1.0 to 6.0 billion barrels of oil in-place remains to be discovered in Permian rocks of the Permian Basin (New Mexico Institute of Mining and Technology 2005). This volume is 1.5 to 9.2 percent of the discovered Permian Basin crude oil.

Deeper, pre-Permian hydrocarbon (mostly gas) accumulations are found in the Delaware Basin and on the Central Basin Platform. Most of the gas is found in structural, stratigraphic, or combination traps that are sealed by shale and impermeable carbonate rocks (Hill 1996). Some Pennsylvanian reservoirs are found near Carlsbad, New Mexico, northeast of the park, but none extend past the northwest-southeast trending Huapache Monocline that intersects the Capitan reef between Rattlesnake Canyon and Carlsbad Caverns (Hill 1987, 1996). The lowermost Pennsylvanian gas reservoir is in the Morrow Formation, about 10,000 feet (3,050 m) beneath Carlsbad Caverns (NPS 1996).

Hundreds of producing gas and oil wells have been drilled north, east, and south of Carlsbad Caverns National Park (figure 4). Exploratory wells have been drilled within a few thousand feet of the north and east boundaries of Carlsbad Caverns, and some of these have encountered voids at the same depth as major passages in Lechuguilla Cave (NPS 1996). At least 61 wells drilled near the park have encountered lost circulation zones in the Capitan and Goat Seep Formations, suggesting that unexplored cave passages were intersected during drilling (NPS 1993, 1996).

Substantial hydrocarbon reserves and known cave resources exist immediately north of the park boundary. It is probable that exploratory drilling will intersect openings that connect with caves in the park. Resources inside the park could be at risk of contamination from toxic and flammable gases and other substances associated with the exploration production of oil and gas.

In 1993, the National Park Service convened a panel of geologists familiar with caves and geology in the Carlsbad region to consider the various risks of contamination to caves within the park from hydrocarbon exploration and production (NPS 1993). The principal conclusion of the panel was that there was no way to protect the cave resources of Carlsbad Caverns without establishing a cave protection zone along the northern boundary.

More detailed information about hydrocarbon reserves and oil and gas production potential in the Carlsbad Caverns area is given in the *Final Dark Canyon Environmental Impact Statement* (BLM 1993) and "Report of the Guadalupe Caverns Geology Panel to the National Park Service" (NPS 1993). More detailed information on the oil and gas resources of the Delaware Basin is available from the oil and gas atlases of the Texas Bureau of Economic Geology in Austin, Texas (http://www.beg.utexas.edu/, access 2005), and the New Mexico Bureau of Mines and Mineral Resources in Socorro, New Mexico (http://geoinfo.nmt.edu/, access 2005).

Sulfur

Sulfur deposits in the Delaware Basin formed in sedimentary rocks by the secondary oxidation of H_2S in groundwater. There are two primary sulfur producing areas in the Delaware Basin: the Rustler Springs sulfur district just south of Carlsbad Caverns National Park and the Fort Stockton sulfur district on the southeast edge of the Delaware Basin adjacent to the Central Basin Platform (Hill 1996). Sulfur also occurs on the Northwest Shelf and in the caves of the Guadalupe Mountains.

Sulfur has been reported in Carlsbad Cavern and Lechuguilla Cave (Hill 1987; Cunningham et al. 1993). Minute amounts of sulfur in Carlsbad Cavern were reported in the Big Room, Christmas Tree Room, and New Mexico Room. In the Big Room, sulfur occurs as an overgrowth crust lining a drip tube in a gypsum block. However, investigators found that some of the material thought to be sulfur was actually the yellow uranium minerals, tyuyamuite or metatyuyamunite (Cunningham et al. 1994; Hill 1996).

Lechuguilla Cave hosts more sulfur than all the other caves in the Guadalupe Mountains combined (Hill 1996). Multi-ton deposits exist in the North and South Ghost Town areas and in the Void. The sulfur has a massive, microcrystalline, conchoidal, or vuggy texture. Ghost Busters Hall, the Rift, the FLI Room, Hard Daze Night Hall, Chandelier Graveyard, and Southwest Branch and Far East sections of the cave are also reported to have sulfur deposits (Cunningham et al. 1993; Hill 1996).

Sulfide, Barite, and Fluorite deposits:

Deposits of various sulfides, barite ($BaSO_4$), and fluorite (CaF_2) are found around the margin of the Delaware Basin in the Guadalupe, Apache, and Glass Mountains and in the Fort Stockton area. The mineral deposits are small and of low economic potential. The mineral deposits in the Apache and Glass Mountains are more extensive than in the Guadalupe Mountains.

In Carlsbad Caverns, barite has been found at several locations within the entrance pit of Lechuguilla Cave (Hill 1996). The entrance lies along a flexure superimposed on the southeastern flank of the Guadalupe Ridge anticline. The barite occurs in the Seven Rivers Formation as an intergrowth with calcite.

Potash

Potash in an informal term usually meaning potassium oxide (K_2O) or potassium carbonate (K_2CO_3), but it may also include a variety of potassium minerals such as chlorides, sulfates, and nitrates with substitutions by magnesium, calcium, and sodium. Encompassing an area of approximately 1,160 square miles (3,000 square km) about 15-25 miles (25-40 km) east and northeast of Carlsbad in Eddy County, the Carlsbad Potash district contains some of the world's major potassium deposits (Hill 1996). At one time, the district supplied about 85 percent of domestic potash production.

Potash minerals occur entirely within the Salado Formation. The Salado Formation was deposited over the Capitan Limestone reef complex, but, in the park area, has since been removed by erosion (figure 3). Only a few deposits have been found outside of the district but are not economic.

Miscellaneous Deposits

Selenite, a clear, colorless variety of gypsum, has been found in the Castile Formation, especially along the small faults in the southwestern part of the East Quadrangle (Hayes 1974). Vast amounts of fine-grained gypsum occur in many areas. Limestone gravel suitable for road ballast has been quarried in the past. Limestone and dolomite from the Tansill, Yates, and Seven Rivers Formations have been used in the construction of the buildings at the park (Hayes 1974).

Paleontological Resources

For many years, geologists have visited an outcrop in Walnut Canyon for excellent exposures of the reef and near-back-reef facies of the upper Capitan Limestone and Tansill and Yates Formations (described in the "Geologic Features" section). Testing the limestone with hydrochloric acid has etched the outcrop and serendipitously exposed many of the marine organisms in the reef. Although fossils occur throughout the park, many geologists recognize the excellent reef exposure in Walnut Canyon as world-class and deserving of special protection. Preservation efforts could model those taken at Dinosaur National Monument to preserve and protect Jurassic dinosaur bones.

Bats and Bat Habitat Management

In summer evenings, about 5,000 bats per minute exit the entrance to Carlsbad Caverns. This evening exodus may last for up to 2 hours. In the early 1900s, an estimated 8 or more million bats were counted at Carlsbad Cavern, but today, only about 300,000 bats (mostly Mexican-freetail bats) use the cave.

There were several very large bat counts in the 1900s, however there are no records of the method by which these numbers were derived therefore they are of questionable scientific value. Although the exact numbers are unsure it is certain that bat populations have declined due to past mining activities, loss of habitat to the expanding human population, and the use of chemicals, especially DDT.

In the 1950s and 1960s. DDT was banned in the United States in 1972, but there is no such ban in Mexico, where the bats spend the winter. In 1994, a large quantity of illegal and improperly stored, DDT was discovered in a shed near the park. This may have contributed to the higher levels of DDT residue in the Carlsbad bats relative to bats in other parts of the country. Two shafts sunk by miners before 1923 also contributed to a bat population reduction. The shafts allowed warm air near the ceiling to escape so that the survival of bat pups in the maternity colony was made more difficult. The National Park Service plugged these shafts in 1981. Bat populations rose to 750,000 in the mid-1990s (Kiver and Harris 1999).

Bats are the only flying mammal in the world and one of the only night predators of insects. These gentle, insect eaters may consume up to 600 mosquitoes per hour and a lactating female can eat over half her weight in insects on her nightly forage. Bats from Carlsbad Cavern National Park are known to eat mostly moths, a significant portion of which are major pests on crops found along the Pecos and Black Rivers. Bats are at the top of the food chain and thus, are susceptible to increased levels of chemical pollutants that concentrate in lower plants and animals. The relationship between the bats, the geology of the caves, and the external environment is a delicate one and accentuates the need for ecosystem management beyond the borders of the park.

Microbes and Lechuguilla Cave

Previously unknown bacteria have been found living on rocks and in pools of Lechuguilla Cave. Surviving hundreds of meters below the ground with no light and no organic input from the surface, these bacteria line the walls, ceiling, and floors of many places in Lechuguilla Cave (Burger and Pate 2001). The pools in Lechuguilla Cave are also teeming with life competing for the few nutrients that exist. On the medical front, enzymes released by the bacteria have been found to attack leukemia cells.

Unfortunately, human exploration introduces foreign bacteria into the cave on skin, hair, and clothing fibers. These bacteria out compete native microbes for food and destroy their populations. To address this problem the park has instituted a policy requiring that everyone who enters Lechuguilla Cave has clean clothes and clean equipment, thus preventing the introduction of microbes from other caves into Lechuguilla. Cave explorers also are required to eat and sleep on drop cloths to catch food, skin, and hair. They are encouraged to wear

bandanas to contain hair and are required to eat their food over plastic bags to catch falling crumbs.

In addition, cavers are restricted from getting near any pools found during exploration. When a pool is discovered, it is reported to the park and to scientists studying the microbes. Scientists approaching the pools wear Tyvek clean suits and set up slides that sit in the cave for up to five years. When the slides are collected, the bacteria are cultured in a lab and studied further (Burger and Pate 2001). Discoveries such as these are significant and demonstrate the need to protect similar natural areas for further research into the microbes and their environment.

Guides and Maps for Interpretation

Printed geologic trail guides are needed for the general public. The guides would also be an aid to the interpretive staff.

Springs associated with the Yates Formation-Tansill Formation contact are the most important water supply for animals in the park. Paul Burger, park geologist, expressed the need to map these springs for all 7.5 minute quadrangle maps (Appendix B). He also expressed a need for geo-habitat maps that associate wildlife habitat with geology, especially for endangered species (Appendix B). There has been no known interest in mapping the surface geology of the park since the 1960s.

Carlsbad Caverns National Park Planning Documents

The 1996 GMP, the 1995 *Cave Management Plan* (CMP), and the 1994 *Resources Management Plan and Environmental Assessment* (RMP) developed programs for the study, protection, exploration, surveying, and monitoring of cave resources. The major programs in these plans are summarized below. Details of each plan may be found in the appropriate document.

Subsurface Resources

The GMP proposes methods to reduce cave resource impacts, including ways to keep people from touching or breaking cave formations and spreading lint from their clothing. The 1993 Lechuguilla Cave Protection Act and the BLM *Final Dark Canyon Environmental Impact Statement* (1993) address cave resources north of the park boundary. The Park Service cooperates with the BLM and the State of New Mexico to mitigate impacts on cave resources within the park's boundary and outside of the park from drilling activities outside of the park boundaries.

The actions that are proposed in the GMP regarding subsurface resources include the following:

- No construction of new buildings or impervious areas (e.g., paved parking lots) above the cavern or other cave resources;
- Install catchment basins in parking lots to trap petroleum byproducts washed off pavement;
- Evaluate the infiltration hazard study;

- Continue to limit visitor access in the Green Lake Room, King's Palace, Queen's Chamber, and Papoose Room to protect the fragile cave resources;
- Increase NPS staff and deploy them more effectively to protect cave resources;
- Emphasize the significance of resources in interpretive messages;
- Implement actions to reduce the impacts of trails on Carlsbad Caverns, including surface material and trail cleaning methods;
- Redesign the trail lighting system to make it more efficient and easier to maintain and to minimize associated algal growth;
- Prioritize research, exploration and mapping needs for Lechuguilla Cave and ensure compatibility with NPS research guidelines and management needs and priorities;
- Evaluate possible improvements to the present Lechuguilla Cave airlock-culvert system;
- Develop a plan for the restoration and rehabilitation of Lechuguilla Cave resources;
- Provide funding and staffing to enforce existing guidelines for exploring and surveying all park caves;
- Protect paleontological resources during cave restoration projects; and,
- Develop a feasibility study to determine if Ogle Cave could be opened for guided tours similar to the tours given at Slaughter Canyon Cave.

The recommendations in the RMP and CMP are consistent with those in the GMP. They include:

- Preserve and perpetuate natural cave systems while providing opportunities for public education, recreation, and scientific study;
- Keep Lechuguilla Cave closed to the general public because of its hazardous nature, unique resources, research potential, and continuing exploration and survey;

- Inventory and monitor all caves designated for regulated public access;
- Provide information packet for visitors to wild caves;
- Photo-monitor caves designated for recreational visitor entry;
- Study water infiltration patterns to better understand and mitigate human-induced changes in the cave ecosystem; and,
- Implement a cave rehabilitation program to offset the alteration of the natural cave environment from over 50 years of intensive human use.

Surface Resources:

The GMP proposes a cooperative plan with Guadalupe Mountains National Park and the Waste Isolation Pilot Project (WIPP site) to monitor air quality in the vicinity of the park. The GMP also proposes to work cooperatively with the state of New Mexico to address water quality issues and to update the emergency flood response plan for flood-prone areas such as Walnut Canyon and Slaughter Canyon.

To protect fossil resources, the GMP proposes evening patrols of the park entrance road to discourage illegal collecting of fossils. Paleontological resources would be inventoried and analyzed. Old and new data is to be incorporated into the Smithsonian Institution's nationwide FAUN-MAP system.

The plan calls for a study of groundwater flow associated with Rattlesnake Springs and an inventory and monitoring of backcountry springs affected by human-made impoundments. The 1989 *Rattlesnake Springs Management Plan* and the 1982 *Water Resources Management Profile* also address water resource protection for the park.

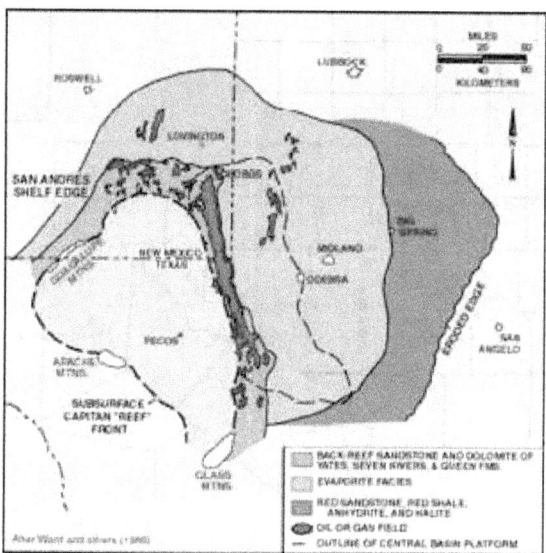

Figure 4. Inferred distribution of depositional facies in the lower Guadalupian strata (A) and upper Guadalupian strata (B) of the Permian Basin. Oil and gas fields producing from those intervals are also shown. Dashed line in (A) represents line of zero net porosity. Diagrams from the New Mexico Institute of Mining and Geology, http://www.geoinfo.nmt.edu/staff/scholle/guadalupe.html#genset (access 2005) and Ward and others (1986).

Geologic Features and Processes

This section provides descriptions of the most prominent and distinctive geologic features and processes in Carlsbad Caverns National Park.

The surface and cave features in the Guadalupe Mountains are the result of geologic forces, climate changes, and the action of water over a vast span of time. The caves in Carlsbad Caverns and in Guadalupe Mountains National Park are the result of a process of dissolution involving sulfuric acid. Decorations in these caves are arguably unsurpassed in the world. On the surface, Carlsbad Caverns NP and the surrounding Guadalupe Mountains provide a unique window to the world's best outcrops of a preserved ancient reef where a 250-million-year geologic story is exceptionally exposed in the desert landscape. The Capitan Reef continues to offer exceptional potential for additional cave discovery, exploration, and research (NPS 1996).

Formation of Carlsbad Cavern

There are 113 known caves within Carlsbad Caverns National Park and most of them reveal the unusual mode of origin by sulfuric acid (H_2SO_4). Most of the world's limestone caves are created when surface water flows down through cracks in limestone and slowly enlarges passageways. Surface (meteoric) water contains dissolved carbon dioxide forming a weak acid called carbonic acid. This acid slowly dissolved the rock in more than 90 percent of the world's limestone caves. These types of caves are typically very wet and have streams, rivers, and sometimes lakes or large waterfalls. They are part of the local or regional drainage system that transports surface water to the sea. This process formed the caves in Mammoth Cave National Park and Buffalo National River in the Ozarks, but not Carlsbad Caverns National Park. There are no flowing streams in any of the hundreds of caves in the Guadalupe Mountains.

About 60 million years ago, during a major episode of mountain building known as the Laramide Orogeny, the central part of New Mexico and Colorado was uplifted, forming a major, north-trending arch known as the Alvarado Ridge. This ridge extended from Wyoming to west Texas and had a maximum elevation in central and southern New Mexico of about 12,000 ft (3,650m). Water in limestone aquifers moved down the east slope of the Alvarado ridge toward Texas, and some of that water flowed through limestones of the Capitan Reef. This water had significant hydrostatic head (pressure) which forced it upward along fractures in the Capitan Limestone to spring outlets scattered through the ancestral Guadalupe Mountains. As water moved upward through the fractures, it dissolved limestone and formed vertically oriented fissure caves. About 30 million years ago, in Late Oligocene to Early Miocene time, uplift culminated in faulting associated with the opening of the Rio Grande Rift along the axis of the Alvarado Ridge. Erosion gradually exhumed the Capitan Reef, and coupled with faulting along the rift, caused the water

table to fall. As the water table dropped, fracture caves became partly air-filled, allowing space for hydrogen sulfide to degas into the atmosphere. Hydrogen sulfide was derived from the microbially assisted alteration of oil and gas and gypsum in oil fields adjacent to the Guadalupe Mountains and is widely distributed in deep groundwater. Once in the cave atmosphere, hydrogen sulfide was rapidly reabsorbed into oxygen-rich water percolating downward from the surface. Mixing of hydrogen sulfide and oxygen in an aqueous environment produced in the sulfuric acid that dissolved limestone and formed the immense passages and galleries characteristic of Guadalupe Mountain caves. Because the Guadalupe Mountains are tilted eastward, the locus of sulfuric acid dissolution migrated eastward with time (DuChene and Cunningham 2006). Consequently, the oldest caves (about 12.5 million years) in the Guadalupes are in the west, and they become progressively younger to the east (3.8 million years at Carlsbad Cavern) (Polyak et al. 1998) (figure 5).

One of the clues, which led geologists to the sulfuric acid hypothesis, is the presence of gypsum ($CaSO_4.2H_2O$) in many caves. Gypsum is produced by the reaction of sulfuric acid with limestone ($CaCO_3$). Gypsum is a soft white mineral that coats walls, and forms crystals in some of the caves. Massive deposits of gypsum in the Big Room past the Bottomless Pit and at numerous locations in Lechuguilla cave attest to the large amount of sulfuric acid required to dissolve the immense rooms of Carlsbad Caverns and other caves in the Guadalupe Mountains.

As dissolution of limestone progressed, support for the cave ceilings was reduced so that ceiling blocks tumbled to the floors of caves. Boulder-size blocks are common, but the largest of them is the massive Iceberg Rock in Carlsbad Cavern that weighs over 200,000 tons (Kiver and Harris 1999). Ceiling breakdown and roof collapse is one hypothesis for the creation of the entrance to the surface (Kiver and Harris 1999). An alternative hypothesis, however, suggests that the entrance to Carlsbad Caverns is a former spring outlet that was fed by water ascending through a tube developed along fractures that extended deep into the Capitan Limestone (Palmer and Palmer 2000).

Speleothems

Many of the speleothems (cave formations) that continue to grow and decorate Carlsbad Cavern are a result of rain and snowmelt percolating through the Capitan Limestone. Surface water contains dissolved carbon dioxide, which makes it slightly acidic and capable of dissolving limestone. Eventually, water saturated with calcium carbonate seeps and drips into the cave where loss of carbon dioxide causes calcite to precipitate as speleothems.

Many cave parks contain the stalactites, stalagmites, columns, flowstone, and helictites that are common in Carlsbad Caverns. However, the park is world famous because of the abundance and variety of common speleothems, and the presence of rare and exotic speleothems, especially in Lechuguilla Cave. Hanging from the ceiling in Lechuguilla Cave are glittering white gypsum chandeliers 15 to 20ft (4.5 – 6m) long, walls encrusted with aragonite 'bushes', and rippling strands of delicate 'angel hair' crystals that may reach 30 feet (9 m) long (Cahill and Nichols 1991).

In the Kings Bell Cord in the Kings Chamber in Carlsbad Caverns, extremely delicate soda-straw stalactites that usually grow to a few inches in length, grow to 6 feet (1.8 m) in length. In Lechuguilla, soda-straw stalactites reach 18 feet (5.5 m) in length.

Stalagmites that grow to immense size are called domes. Giant Dome in the Hall of Giants is 50 feet (15 m) tall. Crystal Springs Dome is one of the few speleothems still growing in Carlsbad Cavern. A thin film of new calcite forms on the surface of the dome as groundwater, saturated with dissolved calcium, drips onto the dome and carbon dioxide escapes into the cave atmosphere. The growth rate for Crystal Springs Dome is estimated to be equal to the thickness of a coat of paint added every 90 years. The size of these speleothems is even more remarkable considering that many grow in a stop and start process rather than a continuous process.

Caves in Carlsbad Caverns National Park also contains subaqueous minerals and speleothems. Elongate calcite crystals ('dogtooth spar') coat some cave walls and one pool in Lechuguilla has clear crystals of selenite (gypsum). Cave pools, many now mostly or completely dry, contain calcite crystals and "pool fingers" that formed under water. Large rounded forms called mammilaries, or "cave clouds" record a time when water filled the cave.

Helictites, distorted twig-like lateral projections of calcium carbonate, remained a mystery to speleologists for many years. Mineralogists discovered a microscopic opening in the center of the helictites that allowed water to move upward by capillary action. Excellent examples of helictites can be seen in the Queen's Chamber of Carlsbad Cavern.

In Lechuguilla Cave, formations similar to conventional helictites were discovered in pools where they are developing under water. Rather than capillary forces, another process known as the "common ion effect" probably formed these features. The pool contains water saturated with calcium carbonate, and it is constantly resupplied with water percolating downward from the surface. Some of this water passes through deposits of gypsum located near the pool, dissolving calcium sulfate in the process. This water, which is saturated with calcium sulfate, flows into the pool. This results in the pool water near the point of influx becoming supersaturated with calcium, which then precipitates to form the worm-shaped speleothems known as

subaqueous helictites (Davis et al. 1992; Kiver and Harris 1999).

Park Caves

Carlsbad Cavern

Carlsbad Cavern is one of the world's largest caverns by volume. It also is considered to be one of the most adorned with speleothems. The paved trail drops about 830 feet (250 m) from the natural entrance through the Main Corridor into the King's Palace area, which includes the Green Lake Room, the King's Palace, the Queen's Chamber, and the Papoose Room. Approximately 750 feet (225 m) below the visitor center, the trail inclines upward to the elevator area (NPS 1996).

The cross-shaped Big Room measures 1,800 feet (550 m) in length, up to 1,100 feet (336 m) wide, and 255 feet (69 m) at its highest point. Various world-renowned speleothems include the Whale's Mouth, the Temple of the Sun, Giant and Twin Domes in the Hall of Giants, the Lion's Tail, Painted Grotto, and Green and Mirror Lakes (figure 6).

Lechuguilla Cave

Lechuguilla Cave is about 4 miles (6.5 km) north of the Carlsbad visitors center. It is the deepest known limestone cave in the United States and contains some of the most spectacular formations in the world. Some of these include subaqueous helictites found nowhere else, rare hydromagnesite (magnesium carbonate) balloons, 20-foot-long (6 m) gypsum chandeliers and gypsum hairs, 15-foot-long (4.5 m) soda straws, and unusual gypsum crystals, flowers, and crusts. The volumes of air entering and leaving the cave during periods of barometric change outside indicate that much of the cave is still unexplored.

Rare chemosynthetic bacteria and obligate fungi, which derive energy from gypsum, magnesium, and iron deposits, have been discovered in Lechuguilla. These organisms are believed to have a role in cave formation, and the pristine conditions of Lechuguilla Cave provide an unprecedented opportunity to study natural cave processes and cave climate. Lechuguilla is within a designated wilderness area and has no human developments above it to alter cave processes.

Over 89 miles (143 km) of passages have been discovered and mapped in Lechuguilla Cave, which may be connected to other known caves outside the park boundary, such as Big Manhole Cave (NPS 1996). Surveyed passages extend within about 600 feet (183 m) of the north boundary of the park. Closed to recreational caving, Lechuguilla is open by permit only for exploration and mapping, limited documentational photography, and research in such fields as cave mineralogy, microbiology, biology, and paleoclimatology.

Slaughter Canyon Cave

Formerly called New Cave or New Slaughter Cave, Slaughter Canyon Cave is one of the larger caves in the park. Located just within the mouth of Slaughter Canyon about 8.5 miles (9.5 km) southwest of the visitors center, Slaughter Canyon Cave is about 1.75 miles (2.6 km) long. The main corridor is approximately 1,170 feet (357 m) long with cross sections up to 220 feet (67 m) wide. The cave is characterized by large rooms with arched ceilings. Parts of the cave are highly decorated with speleothems, including an 89-foot (27 m) column. The hillside above the site contains fore-reef and related fossils.

Ogle Cave

Ogle Cave is connected to Rainbow Cave. The two caves formed independently and are connected by a tight joint passage called Blood Fissure. Ogle Cave is located high on the east side of Slaughter Canyon, across from Slaughter Canyon Cave.

Ogle Cave is one large linear passage about 1,500 feet (488 m) long and averages about 100 feet (30 m) in height and width. The cave is one of the larger chambers in the park. Entry into the cave requires a 180-foot (59 m) technical descent on ropes through a naturally occurring vertical passage.

The cave is decorated with large speleothems. Some of the larger speleothems include massive stalactites, stalagmites, draperies, flowstone, bell canopies, and The Bicentennial column (one of the world's tallest at 106 feet). Smaller speleothems include shields, rimstone dams, cave pearls, helictites, popcorn, and rafts.

Backcountry Caves

Ten of the 84 known backcountry caves are open to cavers with NPS permits. The volume and length of these cave passages vary. Several of the park caves may be interconnected and some may be connected with caves outside the park (NPS 1996).

Caves Outside the Park

The Guadalupe district of Lincoln National Forest contains more than 120 known caves. Most of these are along Guadalupe Ridge just west of Carlsbad Caverns NP. Cottonwood Cave is one of the most prominent with a massive entrance, large formations, almost 3 miles (5 km) of passages, and gypsum deposits in the form of flowers and hanging chandeliers. Other caves include Virgin Cave, Black Cave, Hell Below Cave, Three Fingers Cave, and Madonna Cave.

Several well-known caves are within the Lechuguilla Cave protection area just north of the park. The BLM Dark Canyon special management area is contiguous with the northern boundary of the park. Big Manhole Cave is about 1.25 surface miles (2 km) from the entrance to Lechuguilla and contains deposits of paleontological materials. Big Manhole Cave may be connected with Lechuguilla Cave. Mudgetts Cave and Snake Trap Cave are two other significant caves on BLM land and are close to the park's northern boundary.

Permian Reef Features

The semiarid plateau that surrounds the park is composed of reef limestones deposited between 240 and 280 million years ago during the Permian Period. The Guadalupe Mountains offer a remarkable record of environments associated with this ancient reef complex.

The massive, unstratified limestone reef deposits of the Capitan Limestone form the escarpment seen to the southwest of the visitors center. Unlike modern reefs, which are composed mainly of coral, the primary framework of this Permian reef was made up of calcareous sponges, algae, and bryozoans (figure 7). Skeletal deposits of dead organisms were bound by encrusting organisms and natural calcite cement that filled pore spaces. Today, the preserved reef is approximately 750 feet (230 m) thick. The 1,000-foot cliff, El Capitan, in Guadalupe National Park is composed primarily of the massive Capitan Limestone and most of Carlsbad Caverns lies within this same formation. The ancient reef now preserved in the Capitan Limestone once resembled modern reefs that fringe the coastline of modern Belize in Central America today.

Outcrops in Bat Cave Canyon and Walnut Canyon expose the reef fabric and four significant elements of the reef facies: 1) an *in situ* framework of oriented organisms; 2) encrusting and binding organisms that added stability to the framework; 3) internal sediment of skeletal fragments, pellets, or other grains lodged in open pores in the framework; and 4) submarine cement crusts filling virtually all remnant porosity. (New Mexico Institute of Mining and Geology, access 2005).

The plateaus and canyons that today form the landscape northwest of the Guadalupe escarpment contain the back-reef environments of the Permian reef complex. Features that record the transition from reef to back-reef are exposed in Walnut Canyon. Immediately landward of the reef is the back-reef grainstone facies (figure 8). Strata show signs of open marine circulation, with normal or only slightly hypersaline conditions. Marine fossils are abundant, especially fusulinids and other foraminifers, gastropods, pelecypods, green algae (especially *Mizzia* and *Macroporella*), blue green algal boundstones, oncoids, and other skeletal grains. The carbonates change from massive reef limestone to bedded grainstones and packstones.

Aggregates of round carbonate-coated particles, called pisolites, distinctive features of Grayburg, Queen, Seven Rivers, Yates, and Tansill rocks are found landward of the grainstone facies (figure 8). The back-reef pisolite facies is an elongate feature, parallel to the reef trend exposed in Walnut Canyon and in outcrops along the old guano trail by the cave entrance. As in the Permian, pisolites form today in warm, high calcium carbonate water landward of the reef. They range from a few millimeters to 5 centimeters in diameter).

The Permian pisolitic deposits are associated with large (3-10 ft [1-3 m] high; 30-80 ft [10-25 m] diameter) polygonal features termed "teepee structures" (figure 9) (Dunham 1969; Kendall 1969). Teepee structures are polygonal expansion features marked by buckled and deformed sediments, crusts of precipitated (originally aragonite) cement, and pockets of pisolitic sediment beneath and between the polygonal bulges. They are usually stacked in a series of inverted 'V's. Good examples of teepee structures are found near the bottom of the bat flight amphitheater, and are also exposed in Walnut Canyon.

The pisolites may be the most controversial facies in the Permian of the Texas-New Mexico area (New Mexico Institute of Mining and Geology, access 2005). The origin of pisoliths and tepee structures have been the subject of numerous studies and considerable controversy. Pisolite formation is attributed to one of the following three hypotheses: 1) marine inorganic precipitation in a subtidal setting; 2) caliche formation in continental areas or coastal spray-zones where carbonate sediment is brought in by storms or other episodic processes; and 3) back-barrier, marine or groundwater seepage through permeable barriers into sub-sea level salinas. Adding to the quandary is the lack any modern analog that comes close to modeling the breadth and abundance of pisoliths preserved in the Permian reef complex (Scholle and Kinsman 1974; Esteban and Pray 1977, 1983; New Mexico Institute of Mining and Geology, access 2005).

The persistence of the pisolite facies in space and time, its elongate geometry parallel to the reef trend, and its consistent juxtaposition between open marine and restricted environments indicate that the pisolite facies formed a subaerial barrier between the inner and outer back-reef environments. This scenario would favor either the caliche or salina seep interpretations. Further support for the salina seepage model comes from a number of studies of modern coastal salinas, lakes, and sabkhas in southern and western Australia. Conceivably, an elongate, irregular ridge of low-relief islands, tidal flats, and dunes formed just seaward of the pisolites which allowed marine water seepage into the back barrier lagoon. Exposures in the park allow further testing of all three hypotheses.

Dolomitic mudstones and thin sandstone beds formed in shallow, quiet, and relatively still waters of back-reef lagoons landward of the pisolite facies (figure 8). Dry periods produced mudcracks formed by the buckling of sediments as they partially dried. Mudcracks typically form polygonal structures in a honeycomb pattern. Mudcracks are exposed on the flat ceiling in Carlsbad Cavern near the Bat Cave sign. Modern back-reef lagoons similar to those in the Permian exist today off the coast of Florida.

Back-reef deposits that formed farthest landward from the reef were subject to periodic drying, which concentrated minerals in the water creating extremely saline conditions. Consequently, most marine organisms could not survive in this harsh environment. Most of the fossils seen in back-reef outcrops are gastropods and some types of algae.

Today, semi-permeable clay layers in the Tansill Formation prevent rainwater and snowmelt from easily percolating downward to lower layers. The groundwater accumulates above the clay layers and then moves horizontally until it emerges in springs or seeps along canyon walls. Big Hill Seep, which can be viewed from a pull-out along the Walnut Canyon drive, is one example of this lateral groundwater flow.

The fore-reef environment formed on the ocean side of the reef. As the reef grew upward in the Permian, large house-sized blocks of the reef collapsed or were broken off by waves and fell into deeper water. This process created a poorly sorted debris pile at the base of the reef composed of lime mud, fossils, and reef fragments.

Carlsbad Caverns is developed primarily in the fractured reef and fore-reef Capitan Limestone, but the entrance and all of the upper level are in the back-reef dolomites of the Tansill and Yates Formations. The deep parts of the cave are cut in the lower part of the reef as well as steeply-dipping fore-reef talus of the Capitan Formation. Fore-reef bedding is visible near the Bottomless Pit.

Fossils
Many invertebrate, Permian marine fossils from the Capitan reef system are abundant in Carlsbad Caverns NP. Exposed along Walnut Canyon are, calcareous sponges (e.g., *Guadalupia, Amblysyphonella, Cystaulete,* and *Cystothalamia), Tubiphytes,* stromatolitic blue-green algae, phylloid (leaf-shaped) algae, and bryozoans that form the dominant framework organisms of the reef. Encrusting *Archaeolithoporella* (a possible alga), *Tubiphytes* (found as both framework and encrusting forms), *Solenopora* (a probable red alga), *Collenella* (an algal form) and other, less common, organisms are also seen in the reef facies. Ancillary fauna that lived on the reef and that can be found in the park include foraminifers, ostracods, echinoids, brachiopods, and pelecypods.

Fossil fauna in Walnut Canyon illustrate the change from reef to back-reef environments. These include cephalopods, foraminifers, pelecypods, gastropods, and dasycladacean green algae (particularly *Mizzia* and *Macroporella). Most notably, sponges and encrusting bryozoans are missing.

Modern reefs are commonly formed by large communities of coral, but in the Permian reefs, coral was rare. Solitary horn coral were present but are relatively uncommon in outcrop. Brachiopods were abundant and exhibit a wide variety of shapes. Nautiloids, swimming predators related to the modern chambered nautilus, squid and octopus, are also present. Most nautiloids were extinct at the end of the Permian. Crinoids attached themselves to the seafloor and were common inhabitants in well-circulated Permian reef environments although most species died out at the end of the Permian period.

Two species of trilobites along with the largest fossil sponge yet known from the Permian of North America have been discovered at Carlsbad Caverns (Santucci et al. 2001). Trilobites were among the dominant life forms in the Paleozoic Era but were in decline in the Permian Period and were extinct by the end of the period.

Carlsbad Caverns, Lechuguilla Cave, Slaughter Canyon Cave, and Musk Ox Cave have yielded Pleistocene to Holocene vertebrate fossils. Thirty-six species have been identified from the park caves, and among these species are Pleistocene shrub oxen, pronghorn, an extinct cheetah-like cat, mountain goat, dire wolf, shrew, marmot, horse, and an extinct vulture.

In the Lower Cave and the Big Room within Carlsbad Caverns, fossilized bats, a Pleistocene jaguar, and recent mountain lion bones have been discovered in a location that indicates the animals must have entered the cave by a different route than the present-day entrance (Santucci et al. 2001). In 1947, remains of a juvenile Shasta ground sloth (*Nothrotheriops shastensis*) were discovered in Lower Devil's Den. Additional bones were found in 1959. Dated at 111,900 years B.P., these bones provided the oldest absolute date for any sloth material and the oldest absolute date for any vertebrate remains from the Guadalupe Mountains.

Ringtail cat (*Bassariscus astutus*) fossils are reported from Lechuguilla Cave along with fifteen complete or partial bat skulls. The bat fossils date to less than 10,000 years B.P. and include a hoary bat (*Lasiurus cinereus*) not commonly found in caves, a western big eared bat (*Plecotus townsendii*) that prefers shallow gypsum caves or entrances of caves or mines, a long-legged bat (*Myotis volans*) that prefers rock crevices or trees, and a small-footed myotis (*Myotis leibii*) that was the most abundant inhabitant of Lechuguilla Cave. *Myotis leibii* has not been found at Carlsbad Cavern which is only three miles southeast of Lechuguilla Cave.

Slaughter Canyon Cave (New Cave) is the only cave that has yielded the extinct Constantine's free-tailed bat (*Tadarida constantinei*). Mountain deer (*Navahoceros fricki*) and other vertebrate fossils also have been found in Slaughter Canyon Cave.

Vertebrate fossils discovered in Musk Ox Cave represent an assemblage of Late Pleistocene fauna that died after being trapped in a large sinkhole. A horse, a small artiodactyl, a bovid, a large dog, a bobcat-like feline, a shrub ox, and a small antelope have been identified

among the remains. Further exploration of the cave in 1975 led to the discovery of two skulls and a skeleton that were identified as bush ox (*Euceratherium* cf. *sinclairi*) and dire wolf. A follow-up trip discovered remains of Harrington's Mountain Goat (*Oreamnos harringtoni*) in the cave.

Structural Features

Guadalupe Ridge is a large anticline that dips gently to the northeast. Walnut Canyon occupies a complementary syncline to the north. Bat Cave Draw, situated between the two main east-west passages of the cavern, is a smaller synclinal structure within the large Guadalupe Ridge. Associated with these structures are NW-SE and NE-SW stress-strain trends that influence the distribution and orientation of open versus closed fractures defining the hydrology of the cave system.

Brooke (1996) observed two primary joint orientations: a major orientation of joints between N70°E and N90°E and a second significant orientation between due north and N30°W. Brooke's results corresponded to those found by Tallman (1993) in a regional study of the area, also. Local joints have the same orientation as the major caves. Both joint and cave orientations follow regional structural trends. The dominant joint and cave orientation is parallel to the ridge axis. The second major orientation is perpendicular to the ridge axis (Van der Heijde et al. 1997).

Uplift and folding of the Guadalupe block in Cenozoic time resulted in the preferential joint orientation present today at the park. The continuity, frequency, and hydraulic effectiveness of the joints are controlled and dependent upon the competence of the rock layers and the magnitude of the stresses and strains to which these layers have been subjected. Joints within the massive Capitan Limestone are relatively continuous with some reaching 100 feet (33 m) or more. Fractures in the dolomite and limestone layers of the Tansill Formation, however, are less continuous due to the presence of local siltstone layers.

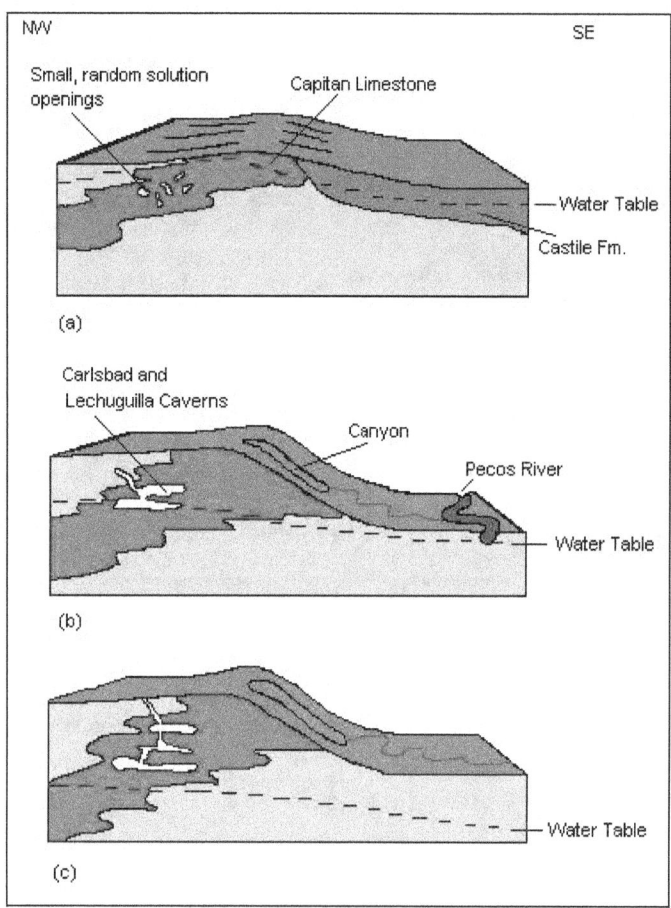

Figure 5. Schematic diagram illustrating the evolution of the cave system at Carlsbad Caverns National Park. A) Small, random solutional openings form in the zone of saturation. B) The water table lowers as the Guadalupe block is uplifted, producing sulfuric acid that dissolves limestone. Caves begin to form. C) Downcutting and cave formation continues as the water table is lowered with continued uplift. Modified from Kiver and Harris (1999).

Figure 6. Speleothems in The Big Room: The Hall of Giants (top) and the Chandelier (bottom). Photos used with the permission of Finley-Holiday Film Corp.

Figure 7. More speleothems in the Big Room, Temple of the Sun. Photo used with the permission of Finley-Holiday Film Corp.

Figure 8. A portion of the diorama of the Capitan reef produced by Terry L. Chase and displayed at the Permian Basin Petroleum Museum in Midland, Texas. This artist's conception emphasizes the framework sponges and the abundant encrusting fauna. Photograph by Peter Scholle, New Mexico Institute of Mining and Geology 1999.

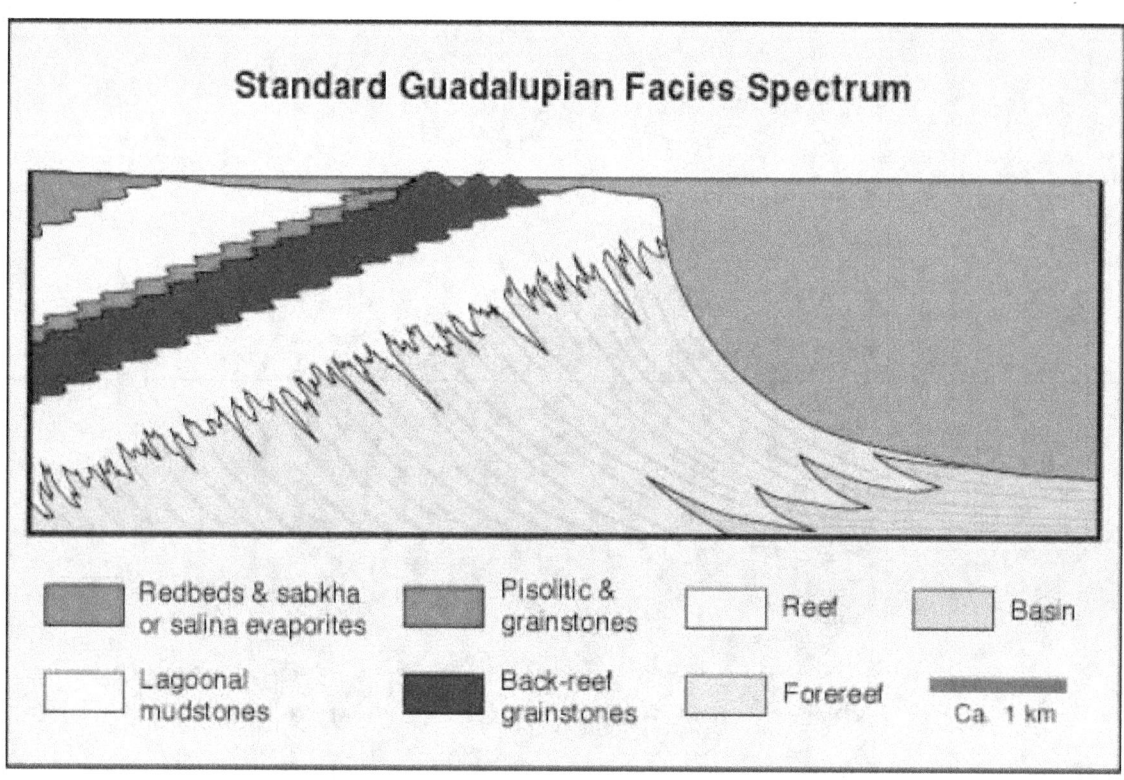

Standard Guadalupian Facies Spectrum

Legend:
- Redbeds & sabkha or salina evaporites
- Lagoonal mudstones
- Pisolitic & grainstones
- Back-reef grainstones
- Reef
- Forereef
- Basin
- Ca. 1 km

Figure 9. Shelf-to-basin spectrum of depositional environments for Capitan and Capitan-equivalent strata of the Guadalupe Mountains. Vertical axis is approximately 0.5 km; horizontal axis is roughly 35 km. Diagram from the New Mexico Institute of Mining and Geology, http://www.geoinfo.nmt.edu/staff/scholle/graphics/permdiagr/GuadPaleogeog.html (access 2005).

Figure 10. Tepee structure in Tansill Formation. Light yellow layers are dolomitized pisolitic and fenestral sediment; darker, gray layers are zones of sheet spar (aragonitic cement crusts). Outcrop at southwest end of parking lot at Carlsbad Caverns visitor's center. Photograph by Peter Scholle, New Mexico Institute of Mining and Geology 1999.

Map Unit Properties

This section provides a description for and identifies many characteristics of the map units that appear on the digital geologic map of Carlsbad Caverns National Park. The table is highly generalized and is provided for informational purposes only. Ground disturbing activities should not be permitted or denied on the basis of information contained in this table. More detailed unit descriptions can be found in the help files that accompany the digital geologic map or by contacting the NPS Geologic Resources Division.

The sedimentary rocks exposed at Carlsbad Caverns National Park are primarily limestone and dolomite that formed in back-reef and reef settings. The following Map Unit Properties Table presents a view of the stratigraphic column and an itemized list of features for each rock unit. Some of the units in the table are correlative so that the geologic column does not represent consistent younger-to-older strata within the Permian Epochs. For example, the Tansill Formation, Capitan Limestone, and Bell Canyon Formation, although geographically distinct, are correlative as are the Yates, Capitan Limestone, and Bell Canyon Formations (figure 3).

Specific properties of the different formations are included in the table that may be significant with regard to management decisions. The properties in the table include the formation name, a lithologic description of the unit, its resistance to erosion, suitability for development, hazards, paleontologic resources, cultural and mineral resources, karst issues, and a miscellaneous category. The units in the table are the same that are on the accompanying digitized geologic map.

Map Unit Properties Table

Period	Map Unit (symbol)	Unit Description	Erosion Resistance	Paleontology Resources	Cultural Resources	Karst Issues	Hazards	Mineral Occurrence	Suitability for Development	Other
QUATERNARY	Alluvium (Qal)	Gypsiferous and calcareous sand & silt. Mapped only in Black River Valley & Dark Canyon.	Low	None	None documented	None	None	None	Groundwater issues?	None
QUATERNARY	Gravel (Qg)	Poorly sorted uncemented limestone pebbles and cobbles from Capitan Limestone and Carlsbad Group; associated silt & clay; some cemented by caliche or travertine; covers much of Castile Fim, esp. north and west of Black River; 200+ ft (61+ m) thick south of Rattlesnake Canyon and west of Black River; 300+ ft (91+ m) thick in wells north of Carlsbad Caverns NP	Low	None	None documented	None	Potential contamination and disruption of groundwater to Rattlesnake Springs	Gravel	Future developments of upper Black River V. could impact flow to Rattlesnake Sp	None
TERTIARY	Dikes (Tb)	Three fine- grained, vesicular, alkali trachyte dikes cut the Castile Fmn secs. 11, 14, & 15, T.26S., R.24E (south of Capitan Ls escarpment; west of Hwy 62); strike about 60 degrees NE; dip about 80 degrees N, 1,000 to 4,000 ft (305 to 1,200 m) long;	Appear as weathered linear zones of brownish soil	None	None	None	None	None	Not exposed in park; limited exposures	None
PERMIAN	Rustler Formation (Pr)	Grayish- pink cryptocrystalline porous dolomite exposed in scattered outcrops south of Capitan Limestone escarpment	Scattered outcrops south of Carlsbad Caverns NP	Dolomite contains mollusks, brachs, normal- marine fossils. Anhydritic parts contain molluscan fauna only	Not in Carlsbad Caverns NP	N/A	None	Halite, gypsum, other sulfates	N/A	May contain the youngest Permian fauna in North America
PERMIAN	Castile Formation (Pcs)	White massive gypsum in the East Quad with some interlaminated white gypsum & dark- gray limestone in the lower part; may include residual gypsum & clastics of the Salado and Rustler Formations in the upper 150 ft; thinly laminated light- to dark- gray granular limestone near the southwest corner and alternating very thin laminae of dark- gray limestone & gypsum in southeast corner of the West Quad; massive white gypsum near mouth of Rattlesnake Canyon	Exposed south of Capitan Limestone escarpment	Non- fossiliferous		Aquitard to groundwater flow	None	Selenite gypsum	Not exposed in park	Springs and seeps
PERMIAN	Tansill Formation (Carlsbad Gp) (Pt)	Light olive gray to very pale orange fine- grained laminated occasionally pisolitic dolomite, mostly in beds 0.5 to 5 ft (0.2 to 1.5 m) thick, & rare thin beds of very pale orange very fine grained quartz sandstone or siltstone; at least 300 ft (90 m) thick near mouth of Slaughter Canyon, normally between 100 and 150 ft (30 to 46 m) thick	High; caps summit of Guadalupe Mtns and over Capitan reef	Gastropods, fusulinids, crinoids, algae near reef		Few karst features	Rockfall potential in canyons	High uranium content (54 ppm); Oil reservoir in Delaware Basin	Local building stone; overlies Capitan Ls caves; exposed in wilderness west of visitors center	World class exposures of backreef features
PERMIAN	Yates Formation (Carlsbad Gp) (Pya)	Very pale orange to yellowish- gray fine- grained laminated frequently pisolitic dolomite, mostly in beds 0.3 to 2 ft (0.1 to 0.6 m) thick, alternating with grayish- orange to pale yellowish orange calcareous quartz siltstone or very fine grained sandstone, mostly in beds 1 to 6 in (2.54 to 15 cm) thick, 270 ft (82 m) thick in North Slaughter Canyon to 375 ft (125 m) thick closer to Capitan Limestone	Slope- forming siltstone & sandstone beds alternating with dolomite ledges	Fusulinids, pelecypods, gastropods, scaphlopods near reef		Low permeable siltstone inhibits groundwater infiltration; some karst	None documented	Oil reservoir in Delaware Basin	Local building stone; exposed in wilderness west of visitors center	World class exposures of backreef features; springs and seeps
PERMIAN	Seven Rivers Formation (Carlsbad Group) (Ps)	Carbonate facies (Psc): yellowish- gray fine- grained laminated frequently pisolitic dolomite mostly in beds 1 to 3 feet (0.3 to 0.9 m) thick with rare thin beds of very pale orange quartz siltstone. Evaporite facies (Pse): white gypsum with associated light olive gray to pale- red aphanitic dolomite & pale reddish brown siltstone; formation thickness: 335-600 ft (110–200 m)	High; Resistant dolomite (overlies Queen Frm)	Fusulinids, pelecypods, gastropods, scaphlopods near reef; fossils rare in evaporite facies		Some karst	None documented	Barite in Lechuguilla Cave; Oil reservoir in Delaware Basin	Local building stone; exposed in wilderness west of visitor's center	Classic example of carbonate to evaporite facies change; springs and seeps

Period	Map Unit (symbol)	Unit Description	Erosion Resistance	Paleontology Resources	Cultural Resources	Karst Issues	Hazards	Mineral Occurrence	Suitability for Development	Other
PERMIAN	Capitan Limestone (Pc)	Massive (reef) Member (Pcm): very light gray to light olive gray, may contain irregularly branching dikes of grayish-orange calcareous quartz siltstone; thickness: 750 to 1000 ft (250–335 m). Breccia (reef-talus) Member (Pcb): foreslope facies; very light gray to light olive gray fine-grained brecciated limestone with widely spaced indistinct bedding planes inclined 20 to 30 degrees to the southeast; thickness: 750 to 1000 ft (250–335 m)	High; cliff former	Reef framework species: calcareous sponges (*Guadalupia, Amblysiphonell, Cystauletes, Cystothalamia*), *Tubiphytes*, algae (blue-green, phylloid, red *Solenopora*), bryozoans; Others: fusulinids, coral, crinoids, brachiopods, cephalopods, pelecypods, echinoderms, ammonoids, mollusks, trilobites; Pleistocene/Holocene vertebrate remains in caves: shrub oxen, pronghorn, mountain goat, dire wolf, shrew, marmot, horse, vulture, cheetah-like cat, ground sloth, free-tailed bat, deer, artiodactyls, bovid, dog	Cultural resources in caves; home to bats	Cavernous, massive, high fracture permeability; speleothems; massive limestone inhibits groundwater flow	Cave collapse; groundwater infiltration may occur along fractures; trails may be slick in caves	Sulfur deposits; uranium minerals (tyuyamuite or metatyuyamunite); gypsum	Development may disrupt bat habitat & impact cave features; exposed in wilderness west of visitors center	World class caves and cave features; unusual mode of origin; most extensive fossil reef on record
	Bell Canyon Formation (Pbc)	Dark-gray fine-grained fetid limestone in beds 1 to 12 in (2.54 to 30 cm) thick & brown-weathering very thin bedded quartz siltstone 3 to 5 feet (0.9 to 1.5 m) thick at top; limestone locally contains abundant silicified fossils; becomes sandstone-rich towards the basin	Not exposed in park; exposed SW of Carlsbad & in GUMO	Bryozoans fusulinids, corals, brachiopods, echinoderms, conodonts, radiolaria, sponges, ammonoids	Not exposed in park	Forereef deposits – no caves in map area	N/A	Oil reservoir in Delaware Basin	N/A	Named for Bell Canyon, a gorge that drains eastward from Rader Ridge to Hwy 62, SW of Carlsbad Caverns NP
	Queen Formation (Pq)	Very pale orange to yellowish-gray fine-grained laminated dolomite mostly in beds 0.3 to 4 ft (0.1 to 1.2 m) thick interbedded with very pale orange silty dolomite, calcareous quartz siltstone, & very fine-grained sandstone in beds 0.3 to 3 ft thick (0.1 to 0.9 m); sandstone is largely confined to the basal part and siltstone is predominant in the upper 100 ft (30 m) (Shattuck Member); ripple marks, cross-bedding, channel cuts in many beds; thickness at type locality is 421 ft (128 m)	Shattuck Member siltstone is relatively nonresistant	Crinoids, echinoids, bryozoans, pelecypods, gastropods, scapholopods, algae near reef; fossils rare in evaporite facies	None documented	None documented	Potential rock fall in canyons west of visitors center	Oil reservoir in Delaware Basin	Exposed on the surface of plateaus in wilderness and NPS land NW of visitors center; upper 1/3 is unstable siltstone	Type section is in Dark Canyon, just below mouth of Payne Canyon (west of visitors center); Springs and seeps
	Goat Seep Dolomite (Pgs)	Thickly-bedded to massive, finely-crystalline to saccharoidal, cream to light-gray dolomite; shelf margin reef dolomite underlying younger Capitan Ls; exposed in extreme SW corner of map area and perhaps Lechuguilla Cave; exposures along Western Escarpment of Guadalupe Mtns from Last Chance Canyon southward; up to 1,300 ft (400 m) thick	High; exposed west of Carlsbad Caverns NP	Sponges, brachiopods, pelecypods, bryozoans, coral, crinoids, echinoderms; (rare) gastropods & ammonoids	None documented	If exposed in Lechuguilla Cave, it is one of only a few caves developed in Pgs	None documented	None documented	Limited surface exposures	Underlies Capitan Limestone
	Grayburg Formation (Pg)	Yellowish-gray to very pale orange laminated fine-grained generally oolitic dolomite mostly in beds 3 to 18 in (7.6 to 46 cm) thick interbedded with yellowish-gray cross-laminated fine-grained oolitic limestone in beds 6 to 18 in (15 to 46 cm) thick, with very pale orange cross-laminated calcareous or dolomitic quartz siltstone or very fine-grained sandstone in beds 4 to 30 in (10 to 76 cm) thick, overlies Queen Fm; basal white sandstone beds form a conspicuous ledge in Last Chance Canyon; about 435 ft (133 m) thick	High; dolomites and sandstones form cliffs	Fusulinid molds (*Parafusulina dunbari*), gastropods, crinoids, brachiopods, pelecypods, nautiloids; algae near reef; fossils rare in evaporite facies	None documented in Carlsbad Caverns NP	None documented in Carlsbad Caverns NP	None documented	Oil reservoir in Delaware Basin	Bentonite layers; exposed west of visitors center in wilderness and NPS land	Type section in Sitting Bull and Gilson Canyons, NW of Carlsbad Caverns NP; Springs and seeps

Period	Map Unit (symbol)	Unit Description	Erosion Resistance	Paleontology Resources	Cultural Resources	Karst Issues	Hazards	Mineral Occurrence	Suitability for Development	Other
	Cherry Canyon Fm. - sandstone tongue (Pcc)	Grayish-orange to pale yellowish orange cross-bedded dolomitic or calcareous very fine-grained quartz sandstone containing abundant silicified fossils; large-scale cross-bedding and channel fillings exposed in Last Chance Canyon; underlies thin San Andres Fm in northwestern part of park; 260 ft (80 m) thick at mouth of Sitting Bull Canyon	Moderately resistant in map area; generally forms slopes	Lower part: fusulinids, echinoid spines, sponges, brachiopods	None documented	None in Carlsbad Caverns NP	None	Oil reservoir in Delaware Basin	Limited exposures in wilderness and on NFS land	None
PERMIAN	San Andres Limestone (Psa)	Very pale orange fine-grained generally cherty fetid dolomite and limestone in even to irregular beds a few inches to several ft thick; mapped in Last Chance and Sitting Bull Canyons Upper Member (Psau) non-cherty, dark, slabby limestone; 100 ft (30 m) thick in Last Chance Canyon, NW corner of map area Lower cherty Member (Psal): cherty limestone; 200 ft (60 m) thick in Last Chance Canyon, NW corner of map area	Resistant to erosion	Common fossils: gastropods, brachiopods, fusulinids, sponges, corals, bryozoans, chitons, scaphopods, pelecypods, nautiloids, ammonoids, trilobites, shark's tooth	None documented	Limited exposures in park - no karst issues	None documented;	Oil reservoir in Delaware Basin, Northwest Shelf, & Central Basin Platform; sulfur deposits in Eddy Co, NM	Exposed NW of visitors center in wilderness and on NFS land	Springs and seeps
	Yeso Formation (Py)	Dolomite, some limestone, red, yellow, & gray siltstone, yellowish fine-grained sandstone, & gray-to-white bedded and nodular gypsum; basal unit thin-bedded, nodular, cherty is interbedded with gypsum; limited exposures in NW part of map	Low	Rare fossils in evaporite sections; poorly preserved brachiopods, bryozoans, crinoids, gastropods, fusulinids in non-evaporite sections		Thin limestone beds: no karst issues		Sulfur deposits in Eddy Co, NM.	Exposed NW of visitors center in wilderness and on NFS land	

Unit descriptions are from Hayes (1974), Hayes and Koogle (1958), and Hill (1996).

Geologic History

This section highlights the map units (i.e., rocks and unconsolidated deposits) that occur in Carlsbad Caverns National Park and puts them in a geologic context in terms of the environment in which they were deposited and the timing of geologic events that created the present landscape.

During the Permian Period (286-245 Ma) (figure 10), the Carlsbad Caverns region was near the equator. Western North America was submerged beneath a shallow tropical ocean while a broad alluvial plain spread across eastern North America. The Appalachian Mountains formed as plate tectonic activity closed the proto-Atlantic Ocean and lithospheric plates collided. As the supercontinent, Pangaea, formed in the late Permian and early Triassic, the proto-Gulf of Mexico also closed as South America collided with what would become the North American continent (figure 11). This collision was responsible for uplift of the Ancestral Rocky Mountains in Colorado.

Active plate convergence caused a rise in sea level, which, combined with regional subsidence, led to the encroachment of a shallow Permian sea into the southwestern region of the North American continent. An arid climate prevailed in the western part of Pangaea restricting marine evaporitic conditions over much of the continental shelf seaway (Peterson 1980).

An arm of this Permian sea flooded into New Mexico and west Texas occupying the Delaware Basin, which had a connection to the open ocean through the Hovey Channel, a narrow channel to the south (figure 2) (King 1948; Hill 1996; New Mexico Institute of Mining and Geology 2005). The Delaware Basin was a relatively deep cratonic basin with depths on the order of 2,000 feet (600 m). The Hovey Channel restricted water flow into the basin much like the Strait of Gibraltar restricts the connection of the Mediterranean Sea with the Atlantic Ocean. Consequently, circulation in the basin was poor and an anoxic environment at depth allowed for the thick accumulation of organic material that later, with burial and maturation, transformed into hydrocarbons.

In the warm, shallow, tropical sea, organic reefs thrived and ringed the Delaware Basin. Depositional environments landward of the reef included redbeds, sabkha evaporites, lagoonal mudstones, pisolitic grainstones, and back-reef grainstones while fore-reef and basin deposits were seaward of the reef (figure 8).

Redbeds, composed of clastic terrigenous detritus, were closest to shore and derived their fine-grained sediments from the north, northeast, and perhaps also the northwest. Sabkha environments formed on the seaward margin of the redbeds and consisted of nodular and mosaic gypsum (sometimes halite) interbedded with some dolomite and red siltstone. This association also is found on modern coastal sabkhas.

Seaward of the main evaporite deposits are fine-grained, thin-bedded dolomicrites deposited in a shallow subtidal or lacustrine setting or a hypersaline marine lagoon (Sarg 1981; Hill 1996; New Mexico Institute of Mining and Geology 2005). Fossils are rare in the tidal flat. Interbedded lagoonal sandstones may represent both fluvial and eolian processes, but probably most are subaqueous deposits. Back-reef lagoons probably were less than 100 feet (30 m) deep and may have been emergent at times, but likely they were never deeper than 3oo feet (100 m) (Hill 1996). Low porosity is characteristic of these strata since pore spaces were plugged with evaporite minerals, especially anhydrite ($CaSO_4$).

Thin (20 cm to 2 m; 8 in to 7 ft) beds of sandstone are interbedded with the dolomicrites. These clastic beds have few sedimentary structures and essentially no fossils or trace fossils. They may represent small progradational advances of sabkha-type sedimentation across the back-reef lagoonal area.

Seaward of the lagoonal mudstones lies the pisolitic grainstone facies. This facies is about 1 mi (1.6 km) wide and about 1 mi (1.6 km) thick (it persists throughout the Grayburg to Tansill section). Irregularly bedded deposits of laminated, fenestral carbonate and beds of skeletal debris are interbedded with abundant lenticular zones of pisolitic dolomite. The pisoids range in size from 0.04 inches to 2 inches (a few millimeters to greater than 5 cm), and although very porous on outcrop, this facies shows extensive filling by evaporite minerals in the subsurface. Associated with the pisolites are teepee structures.

The pisolite facies is always found as a transitional zone between fossiliferous marine grainstones, packstones, and wackestones on the seaward side and the largely barren, evaporitic dolomicrites on the landward side (figure 8) (Scholle and Kinsman 1974; Esteban and Pray 1977, 1983). The consistent geometry and restricted environments of the pisolite facies indicate that at least part of this facies formed a narrow strip of land that was subaerially exposed (except for tidal channels). As such, this facies represents a long-lived barrier to water movement between open shelf and lagoonal settings.

The back-reef grainstone facies lies seaward of the pisolite facies (figure 8). Strata show signs of open marine circulation, with normal or only slightly hypersaline conditions. Marine fossils are abundant, especially fusulinids and other foraminifers, gastropods, pelecypods, green algae (especially *Mizzia* and

Macroporella), blue green algal boundstones, oncoids, and other skeletal grains. The lithology is mostly grainstones and packstones.

The back-reef grainstone facies was a topographically elevated area. Small, coalescing sand waves and islands, perhaps with intervening tidal passes, formed on the seaward edge of this facies and acted as an overall deterrent to water movement farther landward. Unlike the other back-reef facies, the grainstone-island belt underwent only partial dolomite replacement and relatively minor evaporite pore-filling cementation. As a result of their porosity and their proximity to updip, overlying evaporites that plug the pores and prevent the upward movement of liquids, rocks of this facies are often prolific hydrocarbon reservoirs.

Seaward of the back-reef grainstone facies was the main carbonate-producing facies of the area, the reef (figure 8). The Capitan reef was the zone of maximum faunal diversity. Calcareous sponges and phylloid algae formed the major framework organisms of the reef (figure 7). They were encrusted by possible red or blue-green algae. The reef also contained a wide variety of ancillary organisms such as echinoderms (both crinoids and echinoids), bryozoans, brachiopods, mollusks, ostracods, scarce solitary corals, trilobites, and others.

Massive amounts of contemporaneous marine cementation played a major factor in the formation of the Guadalupian reefs. Large and small cavities alike were rapidly filled with carbonate cement precipitated directly from ambient seawater. This cementation reduced porosity to such a degree that the reef facies is not a significant hydrocarbon reservoir despite the fact that locally extensive fracturing has created zones of high permeability.

Unlike today's modern reefs (like the Great Barrier Reef off the Australian coast), the Permian reef probably did not extend into the surf zone. Careful reconstruction of the reef complex suggests that the Capitan Reef, the youngest Permian reef, probably lay a few meters to perhaps several tens of meters below sea level with a more gradual slope into the basin than the sharp reef break of today's reefs (figure 8) (Garber et al. 1989; Hill 1996; New Mexico Institute of Mining and Geology, access 2005).

The rapid rate of marine cementation of the reef facies, coupled with the very high rate of biological productivity, produced more material in the reef margin zone than could be accommodated, given limited rates of subsidence. This excess material was transported into back-reef and fore-reef environments. The Capitan reef of the Guadalupe Mountains prograded seaward between 3 to 6 miles (5 to 10 km) despite sitting at the margin of a nearly 1,800-foot (600 m) deep basin. Such progradation required a very large volume and a high rate of sediment production.

The intense contemporaneous cementation of the Capitan reef, coupled with rapid progradation of largely unconsolidated and compactable debris, led to extensive

fracturing of the cemented reef slab during the depositional process. The fractures formed parallel to the shelf edge and filled with internal sediment, encrusting organisms, carbonate cement, and sand grains.

The fore-reef talus apron is one of the most volumetrically important carbonate facies in the Permian reef complex. Material from the reef, near-back-reef, and upper slope was transported by rock fall, grain flow, debris flow, and turbidity currents and deposited in a relatively uniform apron of steeply dipping rubble. This poorly sorted or unsorted reef detritus varies in size from small fragments and individual constituent grains to larger blocks of lithified reef framework. Bedding angles exceed 35 degrees on the upper slope and gradually flatten to only a few degrees near the basin floor.

Isolated sand-filled channels up to 30 feet (10 m) thick can be found in some areas of the upper and middle slope. Carbonate debris beds interfinger with sandstone beds. The carbonate beds thin into the basin while the sandstone beds, derived from the continent, thicken basinward.

Basinal carbonates are very fine-grained and are generally finely laminated and dark-colored, although organic carbon content rarely exceeds one percent. Basin strata are mostly devoid of fauna except for a few radiolarians. Carbonates are not major constituents of the basin facies but rather, terrigenous sandstones and siltstones provide greater than 90 percent of the basin fill. They have very high porosities in the subsurface and make excellent hydrocarbon reservoirs.

The basin clastics are very fine-grained, subarkosic sandstones and coarse siltstones that are compositionally very similar to the thin clastic units found on the shelf. The presence of abundant detrital sandstone and siltstone in a basin rimmed by a carbonate-producing system posed a significant problem in Permian basin stratigraphy. How were sands deposited in a basin yet leaving so little record in the surrounding shelf-margin facies? The answer was found in stratigraphic features that recorded episodic rise and fall of sea level. Sea level can change due a variety of causes such as regional subsidence, local tectonic effects, eustatic (global) sea level stands, and continent-wide vertical movements.

In the Permian Basin, reefs and/or grainstone shoals flourished during high sea level stands. The platform margins acted as carbonate "factories" and broad carbonate-evaporite lagoons occupied much of the shelf area (figure 12). Thin, but widespread, carbonate turbidite units were deposited in the basins. Clastic sediments were either trapped in vegetated dunes or interdune flats, on sabkhas, or in shoreline deposits well up on the shelf.

When sea level lowered, fluvial and eolian sands and silts spread across the shelf area, accumulating on the margins and eventually transported into the basins to form thick sandstone sequences (figure 12). Some of these sands and silts may also have moved through channels or tidal passes in the barrier reef during times of carbonate sedimentation. This would account for some lenticular sandstone beds, but the cyclic distribution of both shelf and basin carbonate-clastic packages indicates that some form of sedimentation with sea level change is required to explain the overall sediment distribution (Sarg 1985, 1986; New Mexico Institute of Mining and Geology, access 2005).

In very late Permian time, as the final suturing of Pangaea took place, the connection to the open ocean became restricted. Evaporation exceeded the inflow of normal marine water so that salinity increased. With increased salinity, life on the reef ceased. Eventually, thick deposits of gypsum that make up the Castile Formation filled the Delaware Basin and covered the reef core.

Water depths continued to decrease and conditions became even more hypersaline as anhydrite, halite (NaCl), sylvite (KCl), and other evaporitic minerals of the Salado Formation were deposited. Commercial deposits of potash minerals have been exploited in these thick, last-stage fillings of the Delaware Basin.

For most of the Mesozoic Era (figure 10), the Permian Basin region was part of a stable, largely non-depositional province. During the late Cretaceous to mid-Tertiary Laramide Orogeny, the Guadalupe Mountains were locally uplifted accompanied by faulting and southeastward tilting. Karst development may have begun at higher elevations. Sediment eroded from the higher regions may have filled any remaining karst features of Permian age at lower elevations. Tectonic activity may have mobilized hydrogen sulfide gas and

sulfide-rich brines in mid-Tertiary time, producing sulfuric acid by mixing with oxygenated water infiltrating from the surface. Carlsbad Cavern began to form within the phreatic (saturated) zone although the extent of its development at this time is not yet known.

During the late Cenozoic (1-3 Ma), the region was uplifted and the Guadalupe Mountains tilted to the east-northeast. The caves were further enlarged, and extensive gypsum was deposited as a result of carbonate dissolution by sulfuric acid. Joints (fractures without significant displacement) reopened parallel to the reef front and a lesser set of joints formed perpendicular to this first set.

Uplift and erosion continued to dissect the region during the Pleistocene Epoch, and the major Guadalupe caves gradually emerged into the vadose (unsaturated) zone. Erosion removed the younger rocks and part of the Castile Formation and exhumed the buried reef front that forms the Guadalupe Escarpment today. Meteoric, carbon dioxide-rich water from the surface deposited travertine speleothems, particularly during times of humid climate in the Pleistocene. Age dates from the Big Room indicate that Carlsbad Cavern was drained at that level more than 500,000 to 600,000 years ago.

Eventually, erosion exposed the upper cave level and formed the entrance of Carlsbad Cavern. With drying of the cave and a decrease in infiltrating water in the semiarid climate, the rate of speleothem growth decreased. Today, Quaternary-age gravel and alluvial deposits continue to be deposited in the canyons along Guadalupe Ridge

Eon	Era	Period	Epoch		Life Forms	N. American Tectonics
Phanerozoic (Phaneros = "evident", zoic = "life")	Cenozoic	Quaternary	Recent, or Holocene —0.01—	Age of Mammals	Modern man	Cascade volcanoes
			Pleistocene —1.8—		Extinction of large mammals and birds	Worldwide glaciation
		Tertiary 23.0 33.9	Pliocene —5.3—		Large carnivores	Uplift of Sierra Nevada
			Miocene —23.7—		Whales and apes	Linking of N. & S. America
			Oligocene —36.6—			Basin-and-Range Extension
			Eocene —55.8—		Early primates	Laramide orogeny ends (West)
			Paleocene			
		—65.5—				
	Mesozoic	Cretaceous		Age of Dinosaurs	**Mass extinctions** Placental mammals Early flowering plants	Laramide orogeny (West) Sevier orogeny (West) Nevadan orogeny (West)
		—145.5—			First mammals	Elko orogeny (West)
		Jurassic			Flying reptiles	Breakup of Pangea begins
		—199.6—			First dinosaurs	Sonoma orogeny (West)
		Triassic				
		—251.0—				
	Paleozoic	Permian		Age of Amphibians	**Mass extinctions** Coal-forming forests diminish	Supercontinent Pangea intact Ouachita orogeny (South) Alleghenian (Applachian) orogeny (East) Ancestral Rocky Mts. (West)
		—299.0—				
		Pennsylvanian			Coal-forming swamps Sharks abundant	
		—318.1—			Variety of insects	
		Mississippian			First amphibians First reptiles	
		—359.2—		Fishes	**Mass extinctions** First forests (evergreens)	Antler orogeny (West) Acadian orogeny (East-NE)
		Devonian				
		—416.0—			First land plants	
		Silurian				
		—443.7—		Invertebrates	**Mass extinctions** First primitive fish Trilobite maximum Rise of corals	Taconic orogeny (NE)
		Ordovician				
		—488.3—				
		Cambrian		Marine	Early shelled organisms	Avalonian orogeny (NE) Extensive oceans cover most of N. America
		—542.0—				
Proterozoic ("Early life")		Precambrain			1st multicelled organisms Jellyfish fossil (670 Ma)	Formation of early supercontinent First iron deposits Abundant carbonate rocks
Archean ("Ancient")			2500—		Early bacteria & algae	Oldest known Earth rocks (~ 3.96 billion years ago)
			~ 3800—			
Hadean ("Beneath the Earth")					Origin of life?	Oldest moon rocks (4-4.6 billion years ago) Earth's crust being formed
		~ 4600—			Formation of the Earth	

Figure 11. Geologic time scale showing the various life forms and major tectonic events in North America. Ages are based on the 2004 geologic time scale from the International Commission on Stratigraphy.

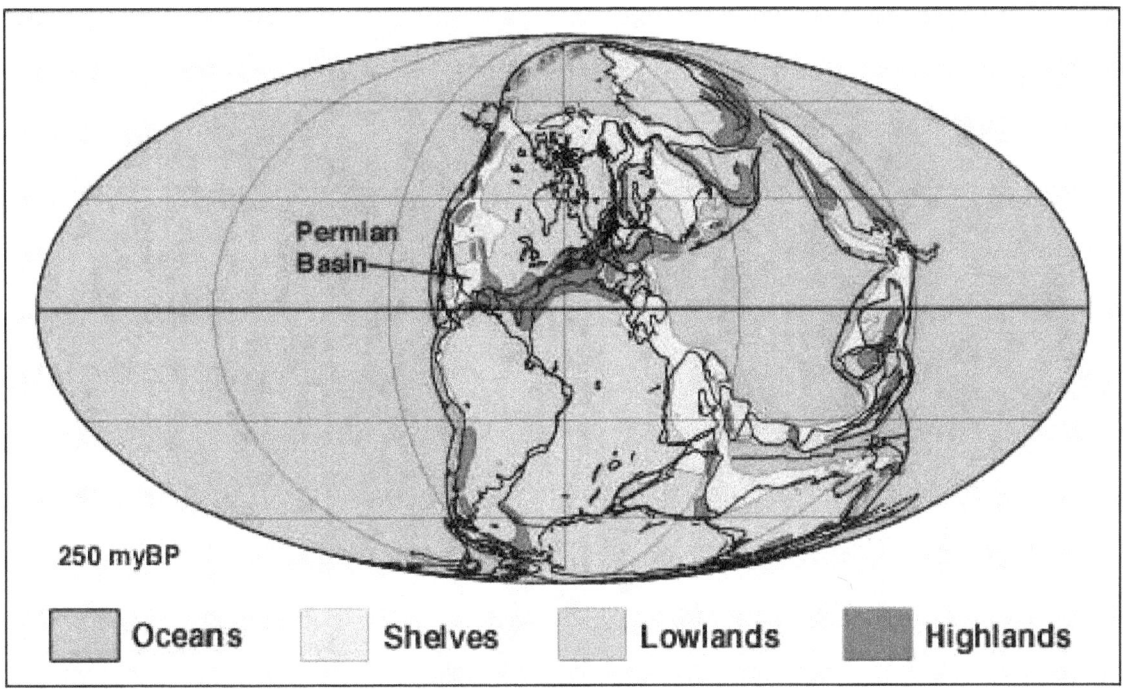

Figure 12. Continental reconstruction during Late Permian (Kazanian) time. In this model, the Permian Basin lies just south of the equator and close to the western margin of the supercontinent Pangaea. Approximate present-day continental outlines shown for reference. From the New Mexico Institute of Mining and Geology, http://www.geoinfo.nmt.edu/staff/scholle/graphics/permdiagr/GuadPaleogeog.html (access 2005) and Scotese and others (1979).

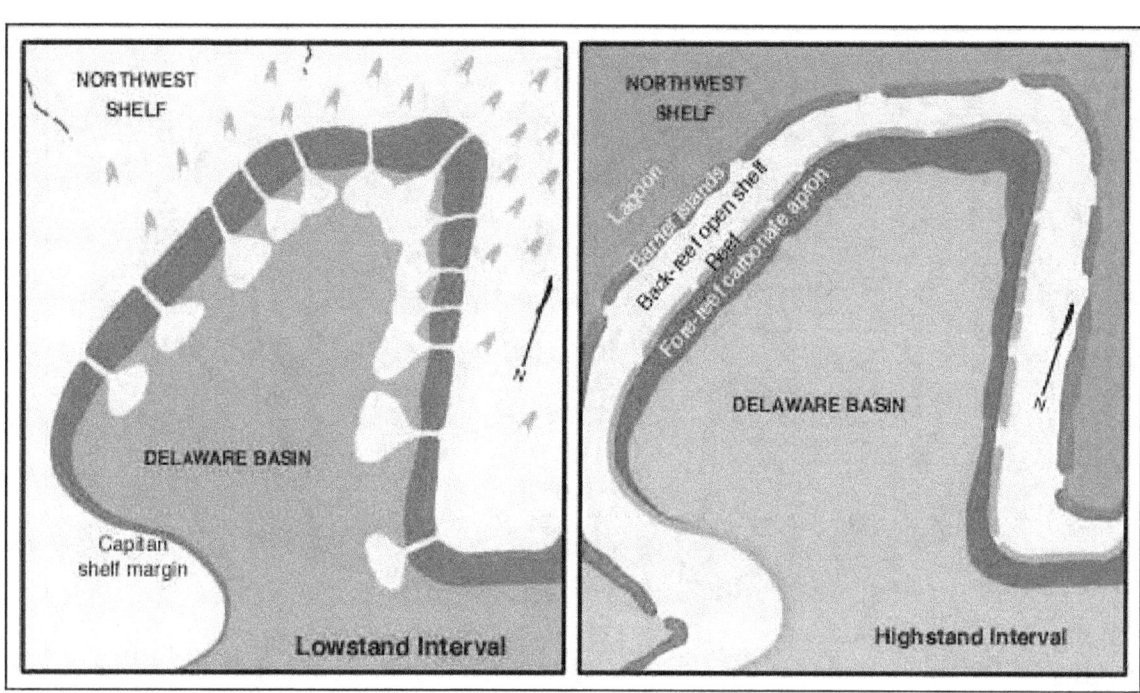

Figure 13. Hypothetical views of the Delaware Basin and surrounding platform areas during sea-level low- and highstands. Lowstand intervals were periods of terrigenous sand transport across shelves, mainly by eolian processes, and sand deposition occurred mainly in the basin. Highstand intervals saw development of shelf-margin reefs with associated back-reef carbonate-evaporite-redbed deposits and thick carbonate fore reef talus deposits. Basins of this time had only thin calcareous shale deposition. From the New Mexico Institute of Mining and Geology, http://www.geoinfo.nmt.edu/staff/scholle/graphics/permdiagr/GuadPaleogeog.html (access 2005).

Glossary

This glossary contains brief definitions of technical geologic terms used in this report. Not all geologic terms used are referenced. For more detailed definitions or to find terms not listed here please visit http://wrgis.wr.usgs.gov/docs/parks/misc/glossarya.html.

allochthonous. Formed far from its present place.

alluvial fan. A fan-shaped deposit of sediment that accumulates where a high gradient stream flows out of a mountain front into an area of lesser gradient.

back-reef. The landward side of a reef; the area and deposits between the reef and the mainland.

basin (structural). A doubly-plunging syncline in which rocks dip inward from all sides.

basin (sedimentary). Any depression, from continental to local scales, into which sediments are deposited.

block (fault). A crustal unit bounded by faults, either completely or in part.

boundstone. A sedimentary carbonate rock whose original components (e.g., skeletal matter, algae, foraminifera, etc.) were bound together during deposition.

breccia. A coarse-grained, generally unsorted, sedimentary rock made up of cemented angular clasts.

calcareous. A rock or sediment containing calcium carbonate.

carbonaceous. A rock or sediment with considerable carbon, esp. organics, hydrocarbons, or coal.

chemical weathering. The dissolution or chemical breakdown of minerals at Earth's surface via reaction with water, air, or dissolved substances.

clastic. Rock or sediment made of fragments or pre-existing rocks.

craton. The relatively old and geologically stable interior of a continent.

cross-bedding. Uniform to highly-varied sets of inclined sedimentary beds deposited by wind or water that indicate distinctive flow conditions.

dip. The angle between a structural surface and a horizontal reference plane measured normal to their line of intersection.

dolomicrite. A sedimentary rock consisting of clay sized dolomite crystals

dune. A low mound or ridge of sediment, usually sand, deposited by wind.

eolian. Formed, eroded, or deposited by or related to the action of the wind.

evaporite. Chemically precipitated mineral(s) formed by the evaporation of solute-rich.

facies (sedimentary). The depositional or environmental conditions reflected in the sedimentary structures, mineralogy, fossils, etc. of a sedimentary rock.

fault. A subplanar break in rock along which relative movement occurs between the two sides.

fore-reef. The seaward side of a reef.

grainstone. A mud-free (<1%), grain-supported, carbonate sedimentary rock.

karst topography. Topography formed by the dissolution of calcareous rocks.

monocline. A one-limbed flexure in strata, which are usually flat-lying except in the flexure itself.

mud cracks. Cracks formed in clay, silt, or mud by shrinkage during subaerial dehydration.

oncolite. A small concentrically laminated calcareous sedimentary structure formed by the accretion of successive layered masses of gelatinous sheaths of blue green algae, generally less than 10 cm in diameter.

orogeny. A mountain-building event, particularly a well-recognized event in the geological past (e.g. the Laramide orogeny).

packstone. Sedimentary carbonate rock whose granular material is arranged in a self-supporting frame work, yet also contains some matrix of calcareous mud

Pangaea. A theoretical, single supercontinent that existed during the Permian and Triassic Periods (also see Laurasia and Gondwana).

pisolite. A round or ellipsoidal accretionary body commonly formed of calcium carbonate.

permeability. A measure of the ease or rate that fluids move through rocks or sediments.

porosity. The proportion of void space (cracks, interstices) in a volume of a rock or sediment.

prodelta. portion of a delta below the level of wave erosion.

progradation. The seaward building of land area due to sedimentary deposition.

red beds. Sedimentary strata that are predominantly red due to the presence of ferric oxide (hematite) coating individual grains.

sabkha. A coastal environment in an arid climate where evaporation rates are high.

salina. A place where crystalline salt deposits are formed or found, such as a salt flat or pan.

subarkose. A sandstone that does not contain enough feldspar to be classed as an arkose

tectonic. Relating to large-scale movement and deformation of Earth's crust.

terrigenous. Derived from the land or continent.

trace fossils. Sedimentary structures, such as tracks, burrows, etc., that preserve evidence of organisms' life activities, rather than the organisms themselves.

travertine. A limestone deposit or crust formed from precipitation of calcium carbonate from saturated waters, especially near hot springs and in caves.

uplift. A structurally high area in the crust, produced by movement that raises the rocks.

wackestones. Sedimentary carbonate rock whose granular material is arranged in a self-supporting frame work, yet also contains some matrix of calcareous mud.

References

This section provides a listing of references cited in this report. A more complete geologic bibliography is available and can be obtained through the NPS Geologic Resources Division.

Berg, R.R. 1979. Reservoir sandstones of the Delaware Mountain Group, southeast New Mexico, in N.M. Sullivan, ed., Guadalupian Delaware Mountain Group of West Texas and Southeast New Mexico: Permian Basin Section – SEPM, Publication 79-18, p. 75-95.

Bowen, E.M. 1998. Hydrogeology of Rattlesnake Springs: Eddy County, New Mexico: New Mexico Institute of Mining and Technology, M.S. Thesis, 170 p.

Bremer, M. 1998. Preliminary assessment of environmentally-sound methods for treating and or diverting rainwater run-off from parking lots and roads in the vicinity of Carlsbad Cavern: Carlsbad, New Mexico, National Park Service draft report 62 p.

Brooke, M. 1996. Infiltration pathways at Carlsbad Caverns National Park determined by Hydrogeologic and hydrochemical characterization and analysis: Colorado School of Mines, M.S. Thesis, 182 p.

Bureau of Land Management. 1993. Final Dark Canyon Environmental Impact Statement: Prepared by the New Mexico State Office and Roswell District Office.

Burger, P.A., and D.L. Pate 2001. Using Science to Change Management Perspectives at Carlsbad Caverns National Park, in E.L. Kuniansky, ed, U.S.G.S. Karst Interest Group Proceedings, Water-Resources Investigations Report 01-4011, p. 47-51.

Cahill, T., and M. Nichols 1991. Charting the splendors of Lechuguilla Cave: National Geographic, v. 179, no. 3, p. 34-59.

Cunningham, K.I., H.R. DuChene, and C.S. Spirakis. 1993. Elemental sulfur in caves of the Guadalupe Mountains, New Mexico, in D.W. Love, ed., Carlsbad Region, New Mexico and West Texas: New Mexico Geological Society, Guidebook, 44th Annual Field Conference, p. 129-136.

Cunningham, K.I., H.R. DuChene, C.S. Spirakis, and J.S. McLean. 1994. elemental sulfur in caves of Guadalupe Mountains, New Mexico (abs.), in I.D. Sasowsky and M.V. Palmer, Breakthroughs in Karst Geomicrobiology and Redox Chemistry: Karst Waters Instit. Spec. Publ. I, Abs. And Field Trip guide, Colorado Springs, p. 11-12.

Davis, D.G., A.N. Palmer, and M.V. Palmer. 1992. Extraordinary subaqueous speleothems in Lechuguilla Cave, New Mexico: National Speleological Society Bulletin, v. 52, p. 70-86.

Dolton, G.L., A.B. Coury, S.E. Frezon, K. Robinson, K.L. Varnes, J.M. Wunder, and R.W. Allen. 1979. Estimates of undiscovered oil and gas, Permian Basin, west Texas and southeast New Mexico: U.S.G.S. Open-file Report 79-838, 118 p.

DuChene, H.R. and K.I. Cunningham. 2006. Tectonic Influences on Speleogenesis in the Guadalupe Mountains, New Mexico and Texas: New Mexico Geological Society Guidebook, 57th Field Conference, Caves and Karst of Southeastern New Mexico, p. 211-218.

Dunham, R.J. 1969. Vadose pisolite in the Capitan reef (Permian), New Mexico and Texas, in Friedman, G.M., ed., Depositional Environments in Carbonate Rocks: Tulsa, OK, SEPM Special Publication 14, p. 182-191.

Esteban, M., and L.C. Pray. 1977. Origin of the pisolite facies of the shelf crest, in Hileman, M.E., and Mazzullo, S.J., eds., Upper Guadalupian Facies, Permian Reef Complex, Guadalupe Mountains, New Mexico and West Texas (1977 Field Conference Guidebook): Midland, TX, Permian Basin Section-SEPM Publication 77-16, p. 479-486

Esteban, M. and L.C. Pray. 1983. Pisoids and pisolite facies (Permian), Guadalupe Mountains, New Mexico and West Texas, in T.M. Peryt, ed., Coated Grains: Springer-Verlag, Berlin, p. 503-537.

Garber, R.A., G.A. Grover, and P.M. Harris. 1989. Geology of the Capitan shelf margin – subsurface data from the northern Delaware Basin, in P.M. Harris and G.A. Grover, eds., Subsurface and outcrop examination of the Capitan shelf margin, northern Delaware Basin: Society of Economic Paleontology and Mineralogy (SEPM), Core Workshop no. 13, San Antonio, TX, p. 3-269.

Hayes, P.T. 1974. Geology of the Carlsbad Caverns East Quadrangle, New Mexico: U.S.G.S. Map GQ-98, scale 1:62,500.

Hayes, P.T., and R.L. Koogle. 1958. Geology of the Carlsbad Caverns West Quadrangle, New Mexico-Texas: U.S.G.S. Map GQ-112, scale 1:62,500.

Hill, C.H. 1987. Geology of Carlsbad Cavern and other caves in the Guadalupe Mountains, New Mexico and Texas: New Mexico Bureau of Mines and Mineral Resources, Bulletin 117, 150 p.

Hill, C.A. 1991. Sulfuric acid speleogenesis of Carlsbad Cavern and its relationship to hydrocarbons, Delaware Basin, New Mexico: American Association of Petroleum Geologists Bulletin, v. 74, p. 1685-1694.

Hill, C. 1996. Geology of the Delaware Basin Guadalupe, Apache, and Glass Mountains New Mexico and West Texas: Permian Basin Section – SEPM, Publication 96-39, 480 p.

Jagnow, D.H. 1979. Cavern development in the Guadalupe Mountains: Cave Research Foundation, Columbus, Ohio.

Kendall, C.G.St.C. 1969. An environmental re-interpretation of the Permian evaporite-carbonate shelf sediments of the Guadalupe Mountains: Geological Society of America Bulletin, v. 80, p. 2503-2526.

King, P.B. 1948. Geology of the southern Guadalupe Mountains, Texas: U.S.G.S. Professional Paper 215, 183 p.

Kiver, E.P. and D.V. Harris. 1999. Geology of U.S. Parklands: John Wiley & Sons, Inc., New York, p. 177-189.

Lee, W.T. 1924. A visit to Carlsbad Caverns: National Geographic Magazine, v. 45, no. 1, p. 1-40.

Mazzullo, L.J., and B.S. Brister. 2001. Keys to successful Morrow Formation exploration, southeastern New Mexico: Abstract, American Association of Petroleum Geologist Bulletin, Southwest Section meeting, Vol. 85, p. 388.

National Park Service 1993. "Report of the Guadalupe Caverns Geology Panel to the National Park Service," by Harvey R. DuChene, David H. Jagnow, Lloyd Pray, and J. Michael Queen: On file at NPS Southwest Region Office, Santa Fe, NM.

National Park Service. 1996. Final General Management Plan Environmental Impact Statement: US Department of Interior, National Park Service, NPS D-66A, Denver Service Center, Denver, CO, 286 p.

New Mexico Institute of Mining and Geology. An Introduction and Virtual Geologic Field Trip to the Permian Reef Complex, Guadalupe and Delaware Mountains New Mexico-West Texas: http://www.geoinfo.nmt.edu/staff/scholle/guadalupe.html, access November 2005.

Palmer, A.N., and M.V. Palmer. 2000. Hydrochemical interpretation of cave patterns in the Guadalupe Mountains, New Mexico: National Speleological Society, Journal of Cave and Karst Studies, p. 91-108.

Peterson, J.A. 1980. Permian paleogeography and sedimentary provinces, west central United States, in Thomas D. Fouch and Esther R. Magathan, eds., Paleozoic Paleogeography of the West-Central United States: Rocky Mountain Section, SEPM (Society for Sedimentary Geology), p. 271-292.

Polyak V.J., W.C. McIntosh, P. Provencio, and N. Güven. 1998. Age and Origin of Carlsbad Caverns and related caves from 40 Ar/ 39 Ar of alunite: Science, v. 279, p.1919-1922.

Santucci, V.L., J. Kenworthy, and R. Kerbo. 2001. An Inventory of Paleontological Resources Associated with National Park Service Caves: Geologic Resources Division Technical Report NPS/NRGRD/GRDTR-01/02, p. 8-11.

Sarg, J.F. 1981. Petrology of the carbonate-evaporite facies transition of the Seven Rivers Formation (Guadalupian, Permian), southeast New Mexico: Journal of Sedimentary Petrology, v. 51, p. 73-95.

Sarg, J.F. 1985. Permian shelf calcrete, Shattuck Member, Queen Formation (southeast New Mexico) – shelfal expression of Middle Guadalupian fall in sea level: West Texas Geological Society, v. 24, no. 8, p. 8-16.

Sarg, J.F. 1986. Facies and stratigraphy of upper San Andres basin margin and lower Grayburg inner shelf, in G.E. Moore and G.L. Wilde, eds., San Andres/Grayburg Formations, Guadalupe Mountains, New Mexico and Texas: Society of Economic Paleontologists and Mineralogists, Permian Basin section, Publ. 86-25, p. 83-93.

Scholle, P.A. and D.J.J. Kinsman. 1974. Aragonitic and high-Mg calcite caliche from the Persian Gulf — a modern analog for the Permian of Texas and New Mexico: Journal of Sedimentary Petrology, v. 44, p. 904-916.

Scotese, C.R., R.K. Bambach, C. Barton, R. Van Der Voo, and A.M. Ziegler. 1979. Paleozoic base maps: Journal of Geology, v. 87, p. 217-235.

Texas Bureau of Economic Geology, University of Texas. 2005. Project Summary of the Delaware Mountain Group: www.beg.utexas.edu/resprog/ delbas/ summary.htm, access November 2005.

Van der Heijde, P.K.M., K.E. Kolm, H. Dawson, and M. Brooke. 1997. Determining water infiltration routes from structures located above Carlsbad Cavern, Carlsbad Caverns National Park, Carlsbad, New Mexico: International Ground Water Modeling Center, Colorado School of Mines, 88 p.

Ward, R.F., C.G. Kendall, and P.M. Harris. 1986. Upper Permian (Guadalupian) facies and their association with hydrocarbons, Permian Basin, West Texas and New Mexico: American Association of Petroleum Geologists Bulletin, v. 70, no. 3, p. 239-262.

Williamson, C.R. 1979. Deep-sea sedimentation and stratigraphic traps, Bell Canyon Formation (Permian), Delaware Basin, in N.M. Sullivan, ed., Guadalupian Delaware Mountain Group of West Texas and Southeast New Mexico: Permian Basin Section – SEPM, Publication 79-18, p. 39-74.

Appendix A: Geologic Map Graphic

The following page provides a preview or "snapshot" of the geologic map for Voyageurs National Park. For a poster size PDF of this map or for digital geologic map data, please see the included CD or visit the GRE publications webpage: http://www2.nature.nps.gov/geology/inventory/gre_publications.cfm.

Geologic Map of Carlsbad Caverns NP

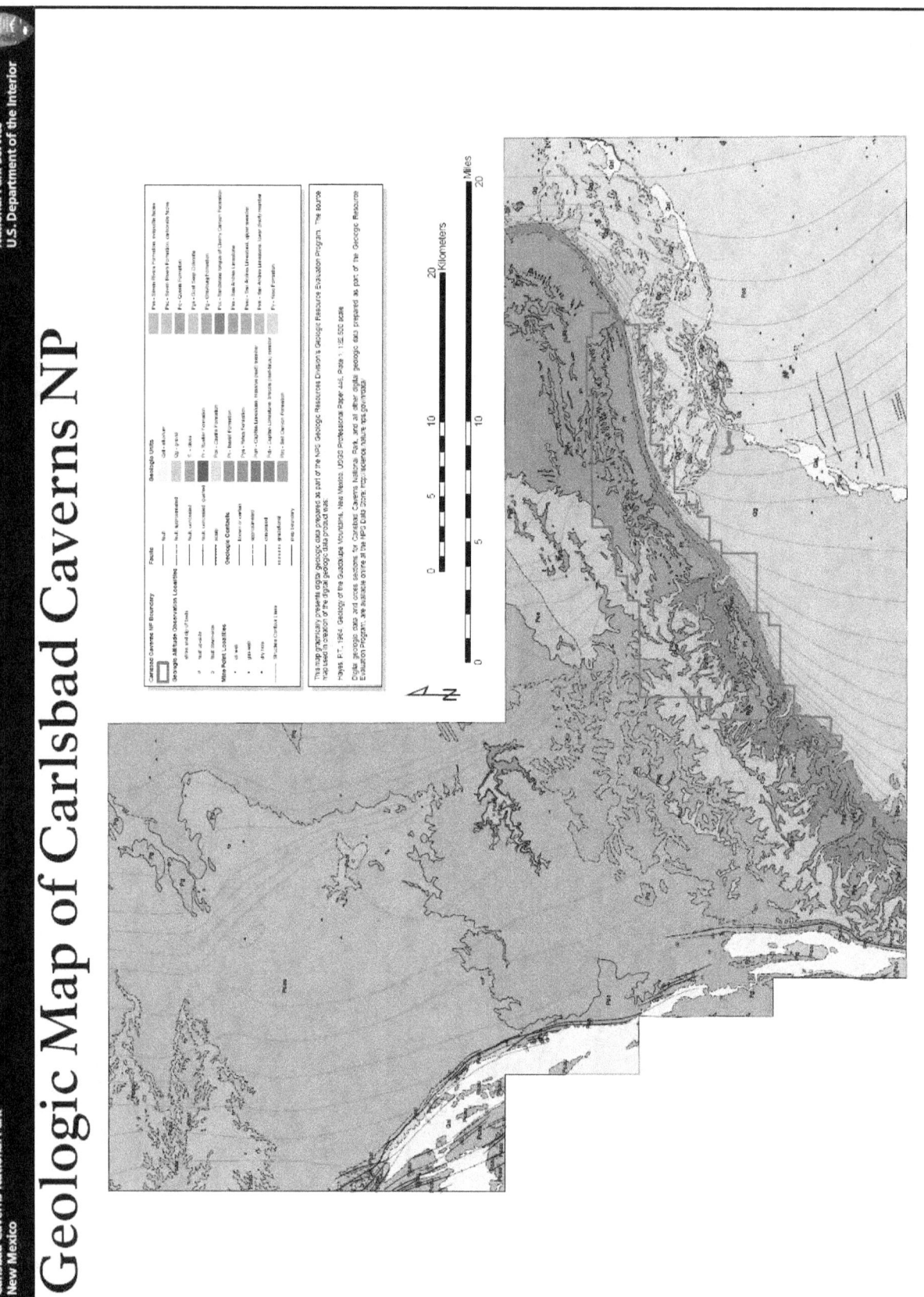

Appendix B: Scoping Summary

The following excerpts are from the GRE scoping summary for Carlsbad Caverns National Park. The scoping meeting occurred on March 6-8, 2001; therefore, the contact information and Web addresses referred to herein may be outdated. Please contact the Geologic Resources Division for current information.

A Geologic Resources Inventory (GRI) workshop was held for both Carlsbad Caverns (CAVE) and Guadalupe Mountains (GUMO) National Parks March 6-8, 2001. The purpose was to view and discuss the park's geologic resources, to address the status of geologic mapping for compiling both paper and digital maps, and to assess resource management issues and needs. Cooperators from the NPS Geologic Resources Division (GRD), Natural Resources Information Division (NRID), Carlsbad Caverns, Guadalupe Mountains, as well as academics from the Colorado School of Mines, the New Mexico Bureau of Mines and Mineral Resources and the Texas Bureau of Economic Geology were present for the workshop.

This involved single-day field trips to view the geology of both GUMO (led by Gorden Bell, Mike Gardner, and Charlie Kerans) and CAVE (led by Paul Burger), as well as another full-day scoping session to present overviews of the NPS Inventory and Monitoring (I&M) program, the GRD, and the on-going GRI. Round table discussions involving geologic issues for both GUMO and CAVE included the status of geologic mapping efforts, interpretation, paleontologic resources, sources of available data, and action items generated from this meeting.

Overview of Geologic Resources Inventory (GRI)

The NPS GRI has the following goals:

1. to assemble a bibliography of associated geological resources for NPS units with significant natural resources; "GRBIB",
2. to compile and evaluate a list of existing geologic maps for each unit,
3. to develop digital geologic map products, and
4. to complete a geological report that synthesizes much of the existing geologic knowledge about each park.

It is stressed that the emphasis of the inventory is not to routinely initiate new geologic mapping projects, but to aggregate existing "baseline" information and identify where serious geologic data needs and issues exist in the National Park System. In cases where map coverage is nearly complete (ex. 4 of 5 quadrangles for Park "X") or maps simply do not exist, then funding may be available for geologic mapping.

After introductions by the participants, Tim Connors presented overviews of the Geologic Resources Division, the NPS I&M Program, the status of the natural resource inventories, and the GRI in particular.

He also presented a demonstration of some of the main features of the digital geologic database.

Geologic Mapping

The USGS has published Professional Papers (PP) on both the Texas and New Mexico portions of the Guadalupe Mountains. PP-215 (by Phil King, circa 1948) covers the Texas portion of the Guadalupes (GUMO) and contains a geologic map at 1:48,000 scale that ends at the Texas state line. PP-446 (by Phil Hayes 1964) covers the New Mexico portion of the Guadalupe Mountains (CAVE) and contains a geologic map at 1:62,500 scale. CAVE staff have supplied GRI staff with a preliminary digitized version of this map that needs some additional attribution. Both were excellent, very comprehensive publications for their day and still are quite useful even though interpretations have been refined since their publication.

The USGS has also published a few other maps that cover the CAVE area. MF-1560-a ("Mineral Resource Potential and Geologic Map of the Guadalupe Escarpment Wilderness Study Area, Eddy County, New Mexico") is mapped at 1:24,000 scale. GQ-112 and GQ-98 are also published as separate maps that predate PP-446 and are both at 1:62,500 scale. Of note, however, is that MF-1560-a only covers the southwestern-most portion of CAVE.

All of these maps were considered worthy of digitizing as they represent some of the best sources of existing "baseline" data. GRI staff will incorporate the digitization of these maps into their future workplan.

Also, the Colorado School of Mines (under the direction of Mike Gardner), has been concentrating their efforts on large-scale mapping of the Permian Reef at GUMO, specifically the Brushy Canyon unit. They have digital versions of this mapping in ArcView format and are willing to share it with the NPS.

Desired Enhancements to the Existing Maps

CAVE 1:24,000 scale mapping: Paul Burger would like to see the six main "quadrangles of interest" for CAVE (Queen, Serpentine Bends, Carlsbad Caverns, Gunsight Canyon, Grapevine Draw, and Rattlesnake Spring) mapped at 1:24,000 scale. At this time, it is not known if Hayes compilation map at 1:62,500 scale was compiled from original 1:24,000 scale maps. If they were, then the data is essentially already there. GRD will attempt to discern if this is true for the Hayes map.

Peter Scholle mentioned that the New Mexico GS will be producing a geologic map of the Carlsbad West quadrangle at 1:24,000 scale, but this is not one of the parks quadrangles of interest, as it lies directly west of the actual town of Carlsbad, which is northeast of CAVE proper. He also thought that the Hayes maps need refinement in the CAVE area.

Paul would also like to see more detailed mapping of the Yates-Tansill contact because it is the location from which water emanates to become the parks water supply.

Suggested improvements to the existing maps

- Refinements to King's maps would involve splitting out the Carlsbad Group into three formations (Yates, Tansill, Seven Rivers formations) to seamlessly edge-match that of Hayes map (and hence eliminate the New Mexico/Texas "boundary fault"). Gorden Bell thought that aerial photography and satellite photos could be used to do this with minimal field checking.

- Integrate Mike Gardner's large scale mapping of the Western escarpment with the King map for better detail for the Brushy Canyon unit members which also include some minor faults that are not shown on King's maps

- Work out the subdivision of the Bone Spring versus the Cutoff formations where the units are shown but the interpretations have changed over time

- Work out the Victorio Peak-San Andres problem which relates to Goat Seep (which is really now known as the Grayburg and Queen);

- Resurveying of roadcuts is desired in and around both parks

- Hazard and rockfall assessments should be conducted, although most susceptible areas don't seem to affect facilities

- Essentially re-map approximately one quadrangle worth of mapping on Carlsbad Group in GUMO (not quad specific); New Mexico Bureau estimates ~$100,000 to do that work

Use of LIDAR technology for higher resolution

Charlie Kerans and Mike Gardner would see the use of LIDAR technology as a great asset to refining any mapping and future research, and would like to have this data available for the Guadalupe Mountains and Delaware Basin in the very near future.

They "rough" estimated the data acquisition at between $60,000 for a "poor-man's DEM" to $100,000 for full LIDAR coverage.

Various ideas were proposed on how to go about accomplishing this task and need to be followed up on by the cooperators. Joe Gregson told the group of the Department of the Interior (DOI) high priority program to obtain funds through regions to obtain such LIDAR information. He mentioned that leveraging with adjacent land managing agencies (Forest Service, BLM, etc) often

is the most successful way to acquire funding for obtaining this technology

Mike Gardner made the suggestion that the Colorado School of Mines, NPS, and Texas and New Mexico Geologic Bureaus cost share to acquire the LIDAR data for the region.

The NPS could not guarantee such funding allocations for FY-2001, but Joe said he would talk to Ingrid Langraf (USGS) about any available funding and would report back to the group at a later time on what he finds out.

Here is what Joe was able to find out as of March 14, 2001:
"At the GUMO/CAVE geologic resources inventory scoping workshop, the group expressed interest in obtaining LIDAR data for the parks and adjacent area to support geologic mapping, research, and resource management. Here is what I found out about getting high resolution LIDAR elevation data for the parks and Delaware Mtns. via the NPS/USGS agreement.

"The USGS does not do a direct 50/50 cost share on LIDAR as with other base cartography but does have contractors available that can fly the area and supply the data. Right now, the ball park cost is about $10K per quadrangle. Contiguous GUMO and CAVE coverage would require about 15-16 quads plus 6-8? quads (guessing) for the Colo. School of Mines (CSM) study area. That puts the project costs in the $200K-$250K range. The best avenue for funding the project (at least for the NPS part) appears to be the Dept. of Interior High Priority Program which annually funds data projects for DOI bureaus. Through the NPS Intermountain Region, CAVE and GUMO park staff can request high resolution elevation data with requirements for LIDAR. If the parks can get other DOI bureaus (BLM, BOR, BIA, USGS, etc.) to also request the data, it has a very good chance of being funded. Unfortunately, the DOI Program call is past for this year, and it runs a year in advance (i.e., a request next year would get put into work in FY 2003 at the earliest).

"I know this does not address the immediate needs of CSM that were discussed at the workshop, but it is the best that I could come up with at the moment. If anyone has other ideas for data sources or funding and wishes to pursue this further, let me know."

Digital Geologic Map Coverage

As stated earlier, it was agreed upon by the consensus of the group that the King and Hayes maps were worthy of digitization with the caveat of the "Desired Enhancements" listed above. Once the maps exist in a digital format they are easier to refine both in the field and electronically.

GRI staff in Denver will attempt to accomplish this digitization in their workplan in FY-2002. Of note, is the existence of digital linework for the Hayes 1964 map in PP-446, but there is no accompanying metadata. GRI staff would also like to get it attributed as per their NPS digital geologic map model. Dave Roemer (CAVE-GIS) will need to be consulted for more specifics on metadata for this coverage.

Charlie Kerans thought that another additional piece of information that should be tied to any digital geologic database would be measured stratigraphic sections that could be georeferenced and brought up in a GIS. This should be easy to add in to the NPS Digital Geologic Database Model.

Other desired GIS data

General needs: Paul Burger would like to see a GIS coverage for linear features for CAVE (Kim Cunningham and Dave Yagnow) for the Dark Canyon Environmental Impact Statement (EIS). Additionally, he is interested in a delineated watershed for Rattlesnake Springs, which is the sole water supply for city of Carlsbad. Ground Penetrating Radar (GPR) or an electromagnetic survey could be used to delineate this.

Soils: Pete Biggam (GRD Soil Scientist) supplied the following information in reference to soils for both parks:

"We currently have in place an Interagency Agreement with the TX - NRCS to map all NPS units in Texas, based upon an estimated completion by 2005 (as funding allows)

"We are estimating that we might initiate soils mapping at GUMO in 2003, and would be utilizing the NRCS soil survey crew that is currently located in El Paso, TX. This, of course, is dependent on funding being provided by NPS I&M for this effort. We would also be looking at initiating soils mapping at CAVE and WHSA in a similar timeframe.

"We operate similar to the GRI, we would schedule a soil scoping session, look at soils research that was already performed at GUMO, map it to National Cooperative Soil Survey Standards with local input from GUMO in regards to their soil resource management concerns.

"Products would be a digital soils map, digital soil attributes, metadata, soil report, as well as potentially some soil information/education products which could be incorporated into GUMO's interpretive program. There would be data that would be utilized within the NPD GIS Theme manager as well, similar to what is being done with GRI.

"We would also have a 'last acre mapped session', where we would have a soils field tour of the park."

Geologic Hazards

GUMO has a published hazards map from R.R. Railsback (University of Texas at Dallas) that was done in 1976. It has been digitized by Parsons Engineering. It is titled *Geologic Hazards in the Pine Springs Canyon area, Guadalupe Mountains National Park*.

Vicky Magnis (NPS-IMR GIS) apparently has this data in digital format from Parsons Engineering and it is currently being tracked down by Tim Connors. It is unknown what format the data is in (AutoCAD, ArcView etc.). Vicki will be working with GUMO staff on the GIS portion of their General Management Plan (GMP).

Paleontology

Greg McDonald (GRD Paleontologist) would like to see an encompassing, systematic Paleontological inventory for both GUMO and CAVE describing the known resources in both parks with suggestions on how to best manage these resources.

Other Sources of Data

- Charley Kerans did a presentation on "Hierarchical Stratigraphic Analysis of a Carbonate Platform, Permian of the Guadalupe Mountains". He mentioned that much of this data will be out in CD-ROM in the near future. It will likely be available from the Texas Bureau of Economic Geology website (http://www.beg.utexas.edu). GRI staff are interested in obtaining a copy of this once it is available to the public.

- The Colorado School of Mines has a website for research on the slope and basin consortium at http://www.mines.edu/Academic/geology/sbc/.

Interpretation

Numerous topics regarding interpretation of geologic resources were discussed. Among these included:

- ·The Permian Reef complex should be better utilized in both parks as the major interpretive focus, and the tie of the Guadalupe Escarpment between both parks should be made to illustrate the importance of the Capitan Reef as a world-class feature that is unique to this area alone. This should also serve to illustrate the GUMO-CAVE story to the regional picture for Permian time.

- Make better use of park trails to showcase and interpret the park geology for visitors

- A Reef diorama in each visitor center showing modern analogs and the process of reef building

- Mike Gardner has offered to assemble a Bone Springs-Shumard trail guide trail for GUMO (for free)

- Make better use of the story of P.B. King's "interpretations" of the reef as a major contribution to the science of geology in general.

Geologic Report

An encompassing report on each parks geology is a major focus of the GRI. To date both the King and Hayes Professional Papers fulfill a major role in describing the regional geology, but are highly technical and not written for the average NPS Resource Manager.

To this end, it was generally agreed that simpler, toned down reports will need to be written for both CAVE and GUMO. The next task is to find enthusiastic report writers to tackle this chore. Both states geologic bureaus (Texas and New Mexico) have offered their assistance in reviewing such reports in final format, supplying maps and graphics on the local geology in their existing publications, and offering their general assistance to the NPS. Peter Scholle says his agency is already doing a publication on the geology of New Mexico's State Parks.

Paul Burger was enthusiastic about writing such a report for CAVE, and thought this would be a good use of his time as the parks geologist.

Jan Wobbenhorst suggested GUMO geologist Gorden Bell as the logical choice to write such a report for GUMO, as he is the local NPS expert on the geology.

Scoping Session Attendees:

NAME	AFFILIATION	PHONE	E-MAIL
Fred Armstrong	NPS, GUMO Natural Resources	915-828-3251 ext. 251	Fred_armstrong@nps.gov
Gorden Bell	NPS, GUMO Geologist	915-828-3251 ext. 249	Gorden_bell@nps.gov
Paul Berger	NPS, CAVE Geologist	505-785-2232 ext. 394	Paul_Burger@nps.gov
Doug Buehler	NPS, GUMO Interpretation	915-828-3251 ext. 105	Doug_buehler@nps.gov
Tim Connors	NPS, GRD	(303) 969-2093	Tim_Connors@nps.gov
Steve Fryer	NPS, NRID	970-225-3584	Steve_Fryer@nps.gov
Mike Gardner	Colorado School of Mines	303-384-2042	Mgardner@mines.edu
John Graham	NPS, CSU	970-225-6333	rockdoc250@comcast.net
Joe Gregson	NPS, NRID	(970) 225-3559	Joe_Gregson@nps.gov
Bruce Heise	NPS, GRD	(303) 969-2017	Bruce_Heise@nps.gov
Charles Kerans	Bureau of Economic Geology Univ. of Texas at Austin	512-471-1368	Charles.kerans@beg.utexas.edu
Vicki Magnis	NPS, IMR GIS	303-969-2962	Viktoria_magnis@nps.gov
Greg McDonald	NPS, GRD	303-969-2821	Greg_McDonald@nps.gov
Dale Pate	NPS, CAVE Cave Specialist	505-785-2232	Dale_pate@nps.gov
Greer Price	New Mexico Bureau of Mines and Mineral Resources	505-835-5752	Gprice@gis.nmt.edu
Dave Roemer	NPS, CAVE GIS		Dave_roemer@nps.gov
Peter Scholle	New Mexico Bureau of Mines and Mineral Resources	505-835-5302	Pscholle@gis.nmt.edu
Jan Wobbenhorst	NPS, GUMO Chief of Natural Resources	915-828-3251 ext. 109	Jan_wobbenhorst@nps.gov

Carlsbad Caverns National Park
Geologic Resource Evaluation Report

Natural Resource Report NPS/NRPC/GRD/NRR—2007/003
NPS D-139, June 2007

National Park Service
Director • Mary A. Bomar

Natural Resource Stewardship and Science
Associate Director • Michael A. Soukup

Natural Resource Program Center
The Natural Resource Program Center (NRPC) is the core of the NPS Natural Resource Stewardship and Science Directorate. The Center Director is located in Fort Collins, with staff located principally in Lakewood and Fort Collins, Colorado and in Washington, D.C. The NRPC has five divisions: Air Resources Division, Biological Resource Management Division, Environmental Quality Division, Geologic Resources Division, and Water Resources Division. NRPC also includes three offices: The Office of Education and Outreach, the Office of Inventory, Monitoring and Evaluation, and the Office of Natural Resource Information Systems. In addition, Natural Resource Web Management and Partnership Coordination are cross- cutting disciplines under the Center Director. The multidisciplinary staff of NRPC is dedicated to resolving park resource management challenges originating in and outside units of the national park system.

Geologic Resources Division
Chief • David B. Shaver
Planning Evaluation and Permits Branch Chief • Carol McCoy

Credits
Author • Dr. John Graham
Editing • Sid Covington, Ron Kerbo, and Melanie Ransmeier
Digital Map Production • Anne Poole and T. T. Hayes
Map Layout Design • Andrea Croskrey